PROFESSIONAL WRITING SKILLS

FIVE SIMPLE STEPS
TO WRITE
ANYTHING TO ANYONE

by Natasha Terk

Write It Well

Corporations, professional association and other organizations may be eligible for special discounts on bulk quantities of Write It Well book and training courses. For more information, call (510) 868-3322 or +65 9648-7727, or email us at info@ vell.com.

Fourth edition © 2014 by Write It Well

Publisher: Write It Well
PO Box 13098
Oakland, CA 94661

Phone: (510) 868-3322

www.writeitwell.com

Author: Natasha Terk

Contributors: Janis Fisher Chan, Diane Lutovich, and Cynthia Owens

Editor: Christopher Disman

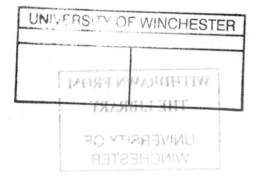

To order this book, visit writeitwell.com.

Our publications include the following books, e-books, and e-learning modules from The Write It Well Series on Business Writing:

> *Effective Email: Concise, Clear Writing to Advance Your Business Needs*
> *Land the Job: Writing Effective Resumes and Cover Letters*
> *Writing Performance Reviews*
> *Reports, Proposals, and Procedures*
> *Develop and Deliver Effective Presentations*

Write It Well offers a variety of customized on-site and online training courses, including the following courses:

> Effective Email
> Professional Writing Skills
> Writing Performance Reviews
> Writing Resumes and Cover Letters
> Technical Writing
> Marketing and Social Media Writing
> Management Communication Skills
> Global Teamwork and Meeting Skills
> Presentation Skills
> Reports, Proposals, and Procedures

Train-the-trainer kits are also available to accompany these courses.

We offer coaching to improve individual professionals' writing and presenting skills. We also offer editorial, layout, and writing services to help authors and teams send out well-organized documents in language that's correct, clear, concise, and engaging.

For more information about any of our content or services,

- Visit writeitwell.com
- Email us at info@writeitwell.com
- Or give us a call at (510) 868-3322

CONTENTS

(CONTINUED)

Why this course?

Communication skills are a vital component of most people's jobs. In any job, it's important to evaluate whether information is worth sending and to send out documents that represent your organization well. It's also important to put yourself in your readers' shoes to keep your information easy to follow. The purpose of *Professional Writing Skills* is to help you make every document clear and engaging — whatever form the document takes, and whoever your readers are.

Remember that you can never be sure how attentive or how distracted people are when they read your documents. Email, text messages, social media, and other forms of electronic communication have led professionals to write more frequently, and our business writing has to compete with a crashing ocean of additional information, entertainment, and ways to connect with others.

It's increasingly important to keep business messages highly focused — offering busy, distracted readers ideas that will register quickly. This book should help you feel confident in your ability to frame an effective message and project a professional image of yourself and your organization, each time you click Print or Send.

Course objectives

This workbook is a self-paced training course, and you'll master these challenges during it:

- Follow a time-tested, five-step planning process to identify your reader, purpose, and main point; answer readers' questions; and organize your ideas logically

- Write a first draft without a lot of redrafting

- Use concise language

- Use clear, dynamic language

- Write email that gets results and saves time for everyone

Lesson overviews

Each of the five lessons in this book includes explanations, examples, questions, and activities that we've designed to help you write more effectively and efficiently.

LESSON 1:   DEVELOP A WRITING PLAN IN FIVE STEPS

Thoughtful preparation makes any business writing more effective, and this lesson outlines five steps to develop a writing plan for any kind of professional document. Your writing always benefits when you put yourself in your readers' shoes and identify what questions they need you to answer.

LESSON 2:   WRITE THE FIRST DRAFT

This lesson shows you how to build a solid document on the foundations you laid during Lesson 1's planning process. You'll review techniques to transition from one topic to another and to format your ideas so that readers will grasp your central point quickly.

LESSON 3:   USE CONCISE LANGUAGE

Long-winded writing sends a dangerous implied message: that you don't value your readers' time. This lesson helps you identify sentence clutter and eliminate unnecessary words from your writing.

LESSON 4: USE CLEAR LANGUAGE

Your readers may move on to other tasks if they find it difficult to grasp your meaning. This lesson helps you write active, specific, straightforward sentences that your readers can follow easily.

LESSON 5: WRITE EFFECTIVE EMAIL

Learn how to write messages that quickly convey just the information your coworkers, customers, and clients need. This lesson will help you use email to save time for everyone and help readers stay focused on the professional needs you share with them.

Getting the most out of this course

Here are four things to keep in mind as you work your way through this self-paced training manual and the exercises in each lesson.

- **USE THIS COURSE HOWEVER IT WORKS BEST FOR YOU.** You could use the five lessons as a workbook, taking notes at the end of each lesson to record your own ideas and strengthen your hold on what you've just learned. Or you might use the table of contents to jump straight to the topic you find most interesting or challenging in your own writing. Review lessons or repeat exercises whenever it seems helpful.

- **USE THIS COURSE FOR YOUR OWN PROFESSIONAL DEVELOPMENT.** The writing tasks in each lesson will help you communicate more effectively as both a team member and a team leader. See the sidebars on pages 18, 24, 38, 45, 51, 81, 111, and 159 for just a few of the ways you can consciously link your written communication skills with your teamwork, leadership, project management, analytical, and other core professional abilities. For further career-development suggestions, see other books in the Write It Well Series on Business Writing, such as *Develop and Deliver Effective Presentations*.

- **CONSIDER EITHER COMPLETING THIS COURSE WITH COLLEAGUES OR USING IT TO LEAD A GROUP TRAINING.** If you're a manager, HR professional, trainer, or team leader, you can purchase this course for anyone in your organization who writes for work. You can also use *Professional Writing Skills* as the textbook for a workshop. (See the writing topics at writeitwell.com for information about our train-the-trainer kits. Or call or email Write It Well for information about how we'd use this manual to deliver an online or on-site workshop for your staff.)

- **APPLY WHAT YOU LEARN TO YOUR OWN WRITING.** Before you begin, gather some samples of your past writing. As you complete each lesson, look through your writing for examples of the problematic language you just learned about. Revising your own writing puts your knowledge in practice and helps you retain what you learn. Furthermore, you'll make sure your knowledge is relevant to the particular communication skills you need for the work you do. The more you practice your writing, the more credible, informed, and professional your image will be.

The purpose of business writing

Each business document should center on a specific purpose, and this fact makes **BUSINESS WRITING** different from other forms of writing. For example, the purpose of **FICTION** is to create a world in which readers can experience such feelings as fear, amusement, loneliness, suspense, joy, and adventure:

> The great Pullman was whirling onward with such dignity of motion that a glance from the window seemed simply to prove that the plains of Texas were pouring eastward. Vast flats of green grass, dull-hued spaces of mesquite and cactus, groups of frame houses, woods of light and tender trees, all were sweeping into the east over the horizon, a precipice.
>
> from Stephen Crane's short story
> "The Bride Comes to Yellow Sky"

This kind of imagination is usually out of place in a professional document, where emotions tend to matter less than practical details such as data, times, goals, and actions.

The purpose of **AN ESSAY** is to stake out a point of view — usually one that doesn't relate to a business need. Here's an author's introduction for an essay on the ethics of eating lobster:

> The enormous, pungent, and extremely well marketed Maine Lobster Festival is held every late July in the state's midcoast region.... Your assigned correspondent saw it all, accompanied by one girlfriend and both his own parents — one of which parents was actually born and raised in Maine.... For practical purposes, everyone knows what a lobster is. As usual, though, there's much more to know than most of us care about—it's all a matter of what your interests are. Taxonomically speaking, a lobster is a marine crustacean of the family Homaridae, characterized by five pairs of jointed legs, the first pair terminating in large pincerish claws used for subduing prey. Like many other species of benthic carnivore, lobsters are both hunters and scavengers. They have stalked eyes, gills on their legs, and antennae.... The point is that lobsters are basically giant sea-insects.
>
> from David Foster Wallace's "Consider the Lobster,"
> *Gourmet* magazine, August 2004

ACADEMIC WRITING has its own fields and rules. Many students write to satisfy the minimum length requirements for a given essay assignment — inflating pages with irrelevant information to make it look as if they've put in a lot of effort. This approach tends to result in long-winded, repetitive documents that are light on meaning and frustrating to read.

This space-filling approach is fatal in business writing. Busy readers need to grasp a message quickly, and they usually have other pressing tasks to finish. Wasting time in a professional document is a quick way to lose your readers' respect.

Looking at samples of business writing can help you get a better handle on the question of how one document should accomplish a specific professional purpose. Read the following email, and then briefly describe its purpose.

TO: **Data Processing Managers**
SUBJECT: Delays in data processing

There's a problem with the Data Processing group, and as a manager, you can help solve it.

The group has failed to meet its deadlines for the past several months, and this failure is causing delays and confusion throughout the company. Please take the following steps:

1. Make sure your team members read the full Data Processing Organizational Format

2. Make sure they follow the format listed on page 23

3. Submit outlines of each team member's responsibilities

When you need to report a problem, follow the procedures on page 603 of the Manager's Handbook.

If you have questions or other suggestions, please email Joe at joe@help. com.

THE PURPOSE OF THIS EMAIL IS _____

_____.

The purpose of professional writing is to help people meet specific business goals by providing them with information they need. To accomplish its purpose, business writing must be easy for the reader to understand. Therefore, the best way to determine whether a business document is well written is to take the point of view of the reader.

PRACTICE

Imagine you're one of the staff members who received this email from Department Manager Kurt Lee. Read the email, and then answer the questions on the next page.

FROM: Department Manager Kurt Lee
TO: FLEC Customer Service Staff
SUBJECT: Email response

We are very fortunate to be in an industry that is expanding. FLEC is the industry leader; we are the largest manufacturer of helix-type FRTs in the world. However, there is no reason to be complacent since our competition is working hard to catch up. We must continue to optimize our opportunities.

Again, I want to thank you and say keep up the good work. Customer service will continue to be important and we have received a larger number of emails than in prior months, and some of the questions about the product are difficult to answer and I understand that it takes some time to figure out who is the right salesperson for each of the clients. I have heard complaints, however, from customers, that they got an automated response from the system but didn't hear back from a sales rep for almost a week. That is unacceptable because our policy is different. I followed up on a couple of these complaints and it looks like our team has been slow to get the messages to the right sales rep; you know, I know that there is a lot going on, but we have a high work load and we need to be as productive as possible!!! If you can't find the right rep, you need to come to talk to me about it because we need to improve these numbers (our customer service guidelines state that anyone who writes should get a personalized message within 24 hours, so let me know if that's a problem). I would like to thank each of you for the extra effort that you have expended as a result of the heavy work load.

Sincerely,
Kurt

PRACTICE, continued

1. Kurt's email includes two long paragraphs. Try to state his main point in one sentence, and ask yourself how easy you find it to identify his main point.

   _____

   _____

2. Could someone have to reread the email to understand what Kurt was trying to say?

   ❏   **YES**   ❏   **NO**

3. What's your image of Kurt as a manager?

   _____

   _____

Turn the page for a discussion of the email.

ANSWERS

1. You may have found it hard to identify Kurt's main point in the email above. He didn't state it clearly, and he buried important information in the middle of the email.

    Here are three possible main points:

    - "You must connect customers to their sales reps within 24 hours."

    - "We need to be as productive as possible."

    - "Thanks for your extra effort."

    Replying to any one of these points could be difficult for a customer service employee because he or she might then seem to be ignoring some or all of Kurt's other ideas.

2. Writers are responsible for presenting information so that readers only have to read it once. It would be difficult to understand Kurt's email without rereading it, and that's a waste of time.

3. Whatever image you have of Kurt as a manager, it's probably not the image he'd like to project. The impression is of someone who lacks focus and isn't a strong communicator. Kurt doesn't seem to have spent much time organizing his ideas, and this impression could make his ideas seem less important. If the ideas aren't important enough for Kurt to organize carefully, why should you spend time reading them?

Suppose Kurt asked you to share some general advice to help plan and focus his writing. Use the space below to list a few suggestions to help him write more clearly—for this email and all his future business writing. One starting suggestion is written in.

My Advice to Help People Plan and Focus Their Writing

- State the main point clearly, right at the beginning.
- _____
- _____
- _____
- _____
- _____
- _____
- _____

Criteria for effective business writing

For business writing to be effective, the writer must take these kinds of actions:

- State the main point clearly, and put it near the start of the document
- Include all necessary information, organize it logically, and omit unnecessary information
- Eliminate unnecessary words and phrases
- Use short sentences and paragraphs
- Use focused, active language and plain English

During this course, you'll learn to write documents that meet all these standards. Covering these bases helps your documents meet three kinds of needs:

- Your organization's needs
- Your own needs as an employee, team leader, or team member
- And your readers' needs for clear, focused, relevant messages

1

DEVELOP A WRITING PLAN
IN FIVE STEPS

OBJECTIVES

In this lesson, you'll learn five steps to plan any kind of professional document.

WHAT YOU'LL NEED:

Picture a document that you need to write for your work — e.g., an email. You'll complete a document plan when you complete Lesson 1, and you can expand your plan into a completed draft in later lessons of the course.

Save time by planning each document

This lesson sets out our **FIVE-STEP PROCESS** to help you plan your writing logically and efficiently:

1. Think about what you're going to write from the reader's point of view.

2. Decide what you want to accomplish: is your primary purpose to persuade readers, or to inform them?

3. Compose a key sentence that expresses your most important message.

4. List the ideas that will accomplish your purpose.

5. Group your ideas into categories.

We designed each step to move you toward a document draft that will advance your professional needs each time you write.

Many business writers allocate their time by the percentages in this chart. What do you notice about it?

THE VALUE OF PLANNING

PERCENTAGE OF TIME	ACTIVITY
5	Think about readers
5	Decide on purpose
5	Identify main point(s)
20	Select information to include
20	Organize information
20	Write quick first draft
20	Revise and edit
5	Proof and correct

Many business writers spend more time planning a document than they do writing it. Especially when you're pressed for time, you may see document planning as a distraction and feel impatient to dive into your first draft. However, initial planning tends to save you time and energy as you draft your ideas.

We've all read material by writers who lose us at some point in the document — sometimes during the opening lines. Here's an example of poorly planned writing:

> Some of the current problems that have been experienced with the current system that have been highlighted are (1) the system has become antiquated and inefficient, (2) which means it currently takes 10 minutes to process a claim. This time can be extended substantially in the case that information has been purged from the source. (3) Limited reporting functionalities also prevent full visibility for past and current claims. The system is in need of updating. Your feedback on this would be appreciated ASAP.

This writer didn't take much time to decide what he or she wanted readers to grasp. What do you think the writer was trying to communicate?

_____

_____

_____

_____

_____

Here's a revision of that paragraph that reflects thought and planning:

> Please give us the approval we need to update the current system, which is antiquated and inefficient. With an updated system, we will be able to streamline claims processing and store documentation so that users can access it quickly and easily.

See how much more clear and streamlined the message becomes?

What are some of the benefits of planning your message? List them here.

- _____

- _____

- _____

- _____

- _____

Turn the page to see some benefits.

Here are some of the benefits you may have listed:

- Fewer miscommunications
- Less time spent clarifying
- Less time spent rewriting
- A more reliable, more professional image
- Getting the results you need

In the Introduction, you saw that successful business writing meets specific criteria for planning and organization. This lesson's five-step planning process helps you meet those criteria for each document you write.

A plan for a document is like a set of blueprints for a house: it establishes a stable, final shape that you can build on safely and easily. The planning process gets you ready to assemble a useful final product: a solid piece of writing that your readers can understand easily.

STEP 1:

THINK ABOUT WHAT YOU'RE GOING TO WRITE
FROM YOUR READERS' POINT OF VIEW.

Communication is a two-way process. The process is only successful when another person understands your message.

When you're face to face with people, it's easy to know when they don't understand. Furrowed eyebrows, a vacant look, and restlessness are all signs that your listeners are confused. Questions for further information show that your listeners are engaged, while questions for clarification mean that you need to back up and rethink how you're explaining yourself.

But when you write, you can't see your readers' faces or hear their questions immediately. One of the best methods to clarify your message is to look at a writing challenge from your readers' point of view.

Writers sometimes fail to communicate clearly because they haven't stopped to consider their readers. Will readers be interested in the information? Do they know anything about the subject? Or will the message make them uncomfortable? It's important to answer these kinds of questions about your readers *before* you start to write.

Here's a common situation: Jillian has just started an important project. She needed several key pieces of information from Alan, who works in another division of her company. So she's sent Alan a detailed email explaining what she needs and when she needs it.

If Alan understands her message, he probably will send the information — or at least let her know if he can't send it yet.

But what if Jillian's message was confusing? List some ways Jillian might learn that Alan does *not* understand what she meant in her email:

1. _____

2. _____

3. _____

4. _____

If Jillian's message wasn't clear, then Alan might send the wrong information, or he might not respond at all. Or he might have to call Jillian to ask what she meant. Jillian will have wasted valuable time — her own and Alan's.

Your readers may be very interested in the subject, only slightly interested, or not interested at all. They may agree or disagree with your message. They may accept you as an authority on the subject, or they may not know how much expertise you have. They may know as much as you know, or they may know nothing at all about the subject. All these factors can affect their responses.

Always try to think about the unique mix of interests and needs for information that each of your readers has. This process usually helps you predict some reader reactions before you start writing. Keeping these likely reactions in mind will help you make your message more persuasive, answer questions your readers may have, and increase your professional credibility.

PRACTICE 1.1

Here are some typical writing situations; identify one situation under each checkbox that's real and current for you.

Below or on some note paper, fill in a scenario that matches one way you write professionally to persuade your coworkers, clients, or customers to take action.

Then fill in a second way you write professionally to pass on information.

❑ **I AM WRITING TO PERSUADE MY READER ...**

- To correct a problem
- To clarify something confusing
- To send me something
- To take another action: _____

❑ **I AM WRITING TO INFORM MY READER ABOUT ...**

- Facts I'm aware of
- The consequences of actions or failures to act
- A likely solution to a problem
- Another topic: _____

After you've chosen the situation, write the name of the person who'll receive your written communication. (If you have more than one reader, list their names or describe the group — e.g., "Landlords of the buildings of the 500 block of Main Street.")

READER NAME(S): _____

Now try to get a clear picture of one particular reader by asking and answering some of the following questions. Add other questions if you think they'll help you picture your reader.

IS THE READER ...

❑ Expecting to hear from me?

❑ Familiar with this subject?

❑ Already interested in what I have to say?

❑ Likely to consider me an authority on the subject?

AND IS THE READER ...

❑ Likely to find what I have to say useful?

❑ Familiar with my views on this subject?

❑ Already committed to a point of view?

❑ Likely to agree with my point of view?

❑ Likely to find my message uncomfortable or threatening?

❑ Likely to need further consideration? (Explain how.) _____

_____

SHOW LEADERSHIP BY UNDERSTANDING YOUR AUDIENCE

Identifying other people's interests and needs can translate into long-term benefits for your career — for instance, by strengthening your **LEADERSHIP SKILLS.** Analyzing your readers' or listeners' needs always makes you a more effective business communicator:

- Understanding different people's interests can help you *motivate* your colleagues or team members in an email, a conversation, or a meeting
- This process can prepare you to *coach or mentor* colleagues when they need to learn new information and you need to share your professional expertise
- And the process can help you *plan and lead effective presentations*, as you identify what a specific audience wants and needs to hear

Never skip Step 1 of the writing process. Remember that you write a business document because you need to communicate something specific to one or more readers. Focusing on each reader is necessary to determine what information will convey your message clearly and help you work together to meet your business needs.

WHAT IF YOU DON'T KNOW YOUR READERS?

What if all or some of your readers are people you've never met, or haven't even talked with on the phone? If you're able to respectfully ask them any of the questions on the preceding page, then ask away. If direct questions aren't possible or don't seem like a good idea, then some educated guesses can help you frame a document for readers whose needs are unknown.

First, consider what you *do* know about the readers, or what you can safely assume. Suppose you're writing a proposal to develop a marketing plan for a midsize company. Suppose that your primary reader is the company president, and she'll be the person who decides whether to accept your proposal.

Imagine you've never met the president because you've been dealing with the head of the marketing team up to now. But you can safely make these assumptions:

- She's busy
- She's interested in how your proposal will benefit the company
- She's concerned about what costs and company resources your marketing plan will call for

Next, consider what you *don't* know. For example, you might have to guess (or ask about) the president's level of knowledge about marketing, as well as what she already knows about this project.

This kind of thinking helps you communicate more effectively by transforming strangers into real people with specific professional needs, interests, and concerns.

ASK THESE QUESTIONS ABOUT READERS

Answering the questions below can help you decide what information you'll include or omit in your document.

1. **WHAT DO READERS ALREADY KNOW ABOUT YOUR SUBJECT?** You need to know how much readers already know before you can determine what they need to learn. For example, some readers will already be familiar with a situation while other readers won't be. In that case, you might include extra background information in an attachment or send the additional information to some readers in a separate message.

2. **HOW WILL READERS USE THE INFORMATION?** Will all your readers use the information in the same single way? Will some of them decide what action to take or decide whether to take action at all? Will they determine whether something was done correctly? Or do they simply need to understand a situation better?

3. **IF YOU'RE WRITING ABOUT A TECHNICAL SUBJECT, WHAT ARE THE READERS' LEVELS OF BACKGROUND KNOWLEDGE?** Will readers understand the terms and concepts you ordinarily use with your colleagues to discuss the subject? Or do the readers need you to explain and present your information in simpler language?

FILL IN STEP 1 FOR A DOCUMENT OF YOUR OWN

Think of a work-related email, letter, or short report that you need to write. Identify the read or readers for your document, answering the questions at the right and making notes here or on your computer. When you're done, enter your answers in the space on page 56. As you work through this lesson, you can use page 56 to complete Steps 1–5 and plan a job-relevant document of your own.

ASK THESE QUESTIONS ABOUT READERS

4. **IS THERE A "SALES PITCH" IN WHAT YOU'RE WRITING** — namely, do you want to influence readers in some way? If so, what are the benefits for readers?

   - Are they ready to say yes?
   - Ready to say no?
   - Are they undecided?
   - What objections or concerns are they likely to have?
   - Is it likely that readers' different agendas will affect their responses?
   - Can you compensate for these agendas?

5. **HOW INTERESTED ARE READERS IN YOUR SUBJECT?** Are you hoping that your document will build interest? What angles of the subject are most likely to boost their interest?

6. **WHAT OTHER POINTS ABOUT READERS ARE IMPORTANT FOR YOU TO CONSIDER?** Do they need your information to do their jobs? Are any readers in a hurry for the information? Is your information likely to surprise them? Could some readers be uncomfortable with your ideas?

IS YOUR READER ...

- ❏ Expecting to hear from you?
- ❏ Familiar with the subject?
- ❏ Already interested in what you have to say?
- ❏ Likely to consider you an authority on the subject?
- ❏ Likely to find what you have to say useful?

AND IS YOUR READER ...

- ❏ Familiar with your views on the subject?
- ❏ Likely to agree with your point of view?
- ❏ Already committed to another point of view?
- ❏ Likely to find your message uncomfortable?
- ❏ Likely to need any clarifications or assurances from you?

STEP 2:

DECIDE WHAT YOU WANT TO ACCOMPLISH: IS YOUR PRIMARY PURPOSE TO PERSUADE READERS, OR TO INFORM THEM?

To get results in business, you must clearly explain exactly what you want to accomplish. Your primary purpose for writing always falls into one of two categories:

EITHER

- to **PERSUADE** your reader to do something,

OR

- to **PROVIDE INFORMATION** that you know and that your readers need.

Always ask yourself whether you need your readers to take any action at all. If so, your primary purpose is persuasive — no matter how much supporting information your document also includes. If you have a request, or if you ask yourself whether you should include the word *please* in your message, then your purpose is persuasive.

Read the following email, and try to decide whether this writer's primary purpose is to persuade his reader or to inform her.

> **FROM:** **Michael Bellows**
> **TO:** **Diane Anderson**
> **SUBJECT:** **Annual sales conference**
>
> I would like you to consider moving this year's sales conference to the Horizons Resort Hotel in Marina.
>
> Horizons has all the facilities we need and has offered us an excellent package (I've enclosed details). Marina is centrally located and is served by all the major airlines. If we sign a contract by January 15, Horizons will give us an additional 10 percent discount on room rates.
>
> Let me know if you need more information. I'd like to confirm conference plans by the end of next week — well before the holiday break.

What do you think the primary purpose of this message is?

❏ **INFORM**

❏ **PERSUADE**

Above, Michael's primary purpose was to persuade Diane to do something: to move the sales conference to the Horizons Resort Hotel in Marina.

Now read the following email, and see if you can tell whether the writer's primary purpose is to persuade the reader to do something, or simply to inform the reader about facts he needs to know.

> **FROM:** Eileen McGuigo
> **TO:** George Blocker
> **SUBJECT:** Three-shift coverage in processing
>
> For the last several weeks, we've been provided with three-shift coverage in the Processing Department. Company employees have covered the day shift and swing shift. A temporary employee has been covering the night shift. The third shift was covered on a trial basis, and it's scheduled to end this week. This arrangement has been satisfactory, and we should continue it.

You may have concluded that Eileen's primary purpose was to persuade George to keep the temporary worker on the night shift. Or perhaps you decided her purpose was to inform George about the way the department has been covered for the last three weeks. Or you may not have been able to identify Eileen's primary purpose.

The purpose of this message isn't easy to grasp, so what would you do if you received it? You might scan it quickly, shrug, delete it, and then move on to another task in your busy day.

Here's another version of the email. Can you identify Eileen's primary purpose now?

> **FROM:** Eileen McGuigo
> **TO:** George Blocker
> **SUBJECT:** Please confirm arrangements for shift coverage
>
> I recommend that we continue our three-shift coverage; please let me know what you decide. The coverage has been working out very well in the Processing Department.
>
> We've met all our deadlines and made the most efficient use of employees' time. That's because we've had company employees cover the day and swing shifts and hired a temporary employee for the night shift.
>
> Thanks if you can let me know this week if we can continue this arrangement.

In the second version of the email, you can easily see that Eileen needs for George to decide whether three-shift coverage will continue in the Processing Department. The primary message is right there in the revised subject line and in the new first and last sentences.

Professional people often have more than one purpose when we write. But if your purposes have equal weight, they can end up competing with one another for your readers' attention. So for each document, it's essential that you make just *one* purpose primary.

It's a little like taking photographs. When amateurs use a camera, we often try to get everything and everybody in the frame. The result? A confusing picture that makes it hard to see what the photographer found interesting or worthwhile.

In contrast, skilled photographers can frame a photo around a single subject. They can draw viewers' eyes to that subject no matter how many other people or things are in the field of view.

When you write, help your readers focus on the most important point by determining your primary purpose for writing beforehand. Here are a few examples:

You write primarily to **PERSUADE** readers when you write …

- An email asking the head office to approve your request for new technology
- A proposal suggesting that a prospective client hire your firm for a project

You write primarily to **INFORM** readers when you write …

- A message to a client explaining the reasons to cancel an insurance policy
- A report detailing the findings for a research project

USE WRITING TO SUPPORT YOUR TEAM OR TEAM MEMBERS

Writing is often critical for successful professional teamwork, and team members and leaders communicate more effectively when they identify their primary purpose for each email or status report they write. **TEAM LEADERS** often need to communicate a clear vision in writing — e.g.,

- To give team members precise information
- To persuade them of the importance of an activity
- Or to pass on clear instructions

TEAM MEMBERS also need to have a clear grasp on the purpose of their emails and reports. A team often works more effectively when its members use writing to highlight a shared purpose — e.g.,

- By requesting further information
- By providing clear, informative progress updates
- Or by persuasively suggesting possible courses of action

Here are two messages on the same subject. Notice how easy it is to recognize the writer's purpose in each message.

EXAMPLE 1: <u>PERSUADE</u> THE READER TO ADDRESS THE MEETING

Dear Ms. Layton:

We suspect that you're very busy, but we would be delighted if you'd agree to be the keynote speaker in early October at the first meeting of our new Glendale Climbers' Club. Please let us know if you'd be available.

Our members would love to hear about your mountain climbing experiences. I know your practical know-how will be of great value to us, and we'd be delighted if you'd read from your book.

We'd like to hold our first meeting on Thursday, October 11, at 6:30 p.m. at the Tiptop Cafe. We could also find another time to accommodate your schedule. Please let me know by August 31 whether you will be available to speak to us in early October.

EXAMPLE 2: <u>INFORM</u> READERS ABOUT THE MEETING

Dear Glendale Climbers' Club members,

We will hold our first GCC meeting on Thursday, October 11, at 6:30 p.m. at the Tiptop Cafe, and we hope to see you there.

Our keynote speaker will be Marybeth Layton, who will share her climbing expertise and read from her book. Many members already own the book; you can either bring yours in for the author to sign or buy your copy on the 11th.

Happy climbing, and we hope to see you at the meeting!

PRACTICE 1.2

Read both messages below and identify each one's primary purpose.

> Alicia —
>
> I'd like to suggest that you prepare and distribute an agenda several days before each monthly meeting.
>
> Without an agenda, people waste time coming to meetings they really don't have to attend. Also, people come unprepared to discuss issues because they don't know in advance what will be covered.
>
> I'd be happy to help prepare or distribute the agendas; let me know anything I could do.

PRIMARY PURPOSE: ❑ PERSUADE   ❑ INFORM

> **TO: Planning Committee Members**
> **FROM: Alicia Delgado**
> **SUBJECT: Monthly planning meeting, August 12**
>
> Here's the agenda for our next meeting. I've listed the topics we're discussing so you can come prepared.
>
> You may skip this meeting if you're not involved in any of the agenda issues.

PRIMARY PURPOSE: ❑ PERSUADE   ❑ INFORM

FILL IN STEP 2 FOR YOUR OWN DOCUMENT

Think back to page 20 and to the document you need to write for work. Decide whether your document's primary purpose is to inform your readers, or to persuade them to take action. Use the space at the right to make some notes about your persuasive pitch or about what information you need to pass on. When you're done here, turn to page 56 and record your writing purpose.

ANSWERS

> Alicia —
>
> I'd like to suggest that you prepare and distribute an agenda several days before each monthly meeting.
>
> Without an agenda, people waste time coming to meetings they really don't have to attend. Also, people come unprepared to discuss issues because they don't know in advance what will be covered.
>
> I'd be happy to help prepare or distribute the agendas; let me know anything I could do.

This writer's primary purpose is to persuade Alicia to prepare and distribute an agenda before the monthly meetings.

> **TO: Planning Committee Members**
> **FROM: Alicia Delgado**
> **SUBJECT: Monthly planning meeting, August 12**
>
> Here's the agenda for our next meeting. I've listed the topics we're discussing so you can come prepared.
>
> You may skip this meeting if you're not involved in any of the agenda issues.

And Alicia's primary purpose is to inform committee members of the agenda for the meeting.

The purpose is clear in both these emails because the writers took some time to decide whether they wanted to persuade or to inform their readers.

STEP 3:

COMPOSE A KEY SENTENCE THAT EXPRESSES YOUR MOST IMPORTANT MESSAGE.

Think of your key sentence as the one you'd shout if you had three seconds to get your most important message across to someone you saw in an elevator before the doors closed.

In a well-written document, the sentence carrying the most important message should be so clear that the reader can identify it very easily. Which of the documents below has a clear key sentence?

DOCUMENT A

Dear Mr. Weller:

Safety is our number-one concern, and our safety record shows that we are all trained well. There is a lot of traffic on the block of Jefferson Street between South Main and Mission. The street sees heavy traffic very regularly, yet its current condition is a safety hazard. The street should probably be widened. That would have tremendous benefits, and we could certainly get the job done. A night permit would allow us to start right away.

DOCUMENT B

Dear Mr. Weller:

I am writing to ask you to give my construction company a noise permit to allow night work on the block of Jefferson Street between Grand Avenue and South Main. The street sees heavy traffic very regularly, yet its current condition is a safety hazard.

Widening the street would have tremendous benefits, and we are ready to work day and night to make the necessary repairs.

We hope to begin work as soon as possible. If you have any questions, please call me at my office.

The key sentence in Document B jumps right out, doesn't it? All key sentences should be this easy to find:

> Dear Mr. Weller:
>
> <u>I am writing to ask you to give my construction company a noise permit to allow night work on the block of Jefferson Street between Grand Avenue and South Main.</u> The street sees heavy traffic very regularly, yet its current condition is a safety hazard.

But what about Document A? The purpose is obviously to persuade Mr. Weller to act, but the message has no clear key sentence, leaving the reader to guess what the writer wants him or her to do. Document A is much less likely to get results.

Writers can neglect to include a clear key sentence for several main reasons:

- They haven't decided what they want to say
- They hesitate to state their main point directly
- They assume readers will be able to follow their thought processes without direct statements

But business readers are busy people. They don't have time to guess what you mean to say, and they can't read minds. It's your job as a professional person to express your most important message clearly, and key sentences are the easiest way to make a professional document's purpose immediately clear.

Here are some examples of key sentences that match the writer's purpose.

TO PERSUADE

You want your reader to do something:

- Please approve the plan.

- We need to start the expansion project.

- We hope to include a gym at the new facility.

TO INFORM

You want your reader to know something:

- The project I'm coordinating will be finished by May 19.

- I am sorry to tell you that your application for an extension has been denied.

- Our needs assessment indicates that two-thirds of your staff would benefit from training.

Consciously crafting a key sentence helps you articulate a given document's purpose and stay focused as you write it. Key sentences make each document much more likely to realize the goal that motivates you to communicate in the first place.

PRACTICE 1.3

Below are two descriptions of professional situations. In each situation, the writer wants to persuade the reader to do something.

Write a key sentence that says clearly what each writer wants the reader to do. Feel free to invent information for each new key sentence.

PRIMARY PURPOSE: TO PERSUADE

SITUATION 1:

Employees are parking in the visitor lot instead of the employee lot, violating our company policy and taking up all the spaces reserved for clients. Visiting clients may have difficulty parking, resulting in wasted time and a less welcoming atmosphere from the moment clients arrive. Office morale and client meetings seem to be adversely affected.

_____

_____

_____

_____

SITUATION 2:

I collect timecards on the first Friday of the month for the work completed for the prior month. Many of you contractors send the reports about a week late, and I can't bill the client until all the reports are in. The policy is that contract workers can't get paid until the client has been billed. If you started sending the report on time, my manager would feel less concern and the accounting office would be able to manage project billing much better.

_____

_____

_____

_____

_____

ANSWERS

Your key sentences probably resemble these two for Situations 1 and 2 above. If your key sentences are very different, be sure they clearly express what the writer wants the reader to do.

1. All employees should park in the employees' lot instead of the visitors' lot.

2. You must complete your timecards by the first Friday of the month to get paid for that month's work.

The key sentences you just composed were for situations where the writers wanted to persuade readers to take action. Key sentences read a little differently when your primary purpose is to inform readers about something. Identify the key sentence or most important message in this example.

PRIMARY PURPOSE: TO INFORM

TO: Staff
SUBJECT: Holiday party

We will hold the holiday party on December 16 at the Redwood Lodge from noon to 5:00 p.m.

The sign-up sheet will be posted in the cafeteria by Friday. This year, we're asking everyone to bring a few cans of food for the food drive instead of gifts.

If you have questions, please call Miriam Belladora at Extension 403. We hope you and your family can attend.

The first sentence in the message is the key sentence. It's usually best if the key sentence leads the document.

Notice that when you're writing to inform, your most important message may actually be a statement of one to three sentences, as it is in this example.

PRIMARY PURPOSE: TO INFORM

Dear Clients:

<u>On June 15, I am beginning a three-month leave. While I'm away, my associate, Annabel Leong, will be managing my projects.</u>

Before I leave, Annabel and I will take the following steps to make everything run smoothly:

- We will review the status of all projects and meet with the project teams

- During the last two weeks of May, Annabel will call each of you to introduce herself and answer any questions you may have

- I will provide Annabel with all the project files so she can answer questions and resolve any problems that might come up

I've enclosed Annabel's contact info; you can reach her by phone or email.
I look forward to working with you again when I return in September.

It's usually best if your main message fits in one key sentence, but two or three sentences are fine if they're concise and easy to grasp.

EXAMPLES OF KEY SENTENCES
WHEN YOU WRITE TO PERSUADE

Here are six situations that call for tactful persuasive writing. When you write to persuade, start by looking for a mutual goal — e.g., to complete a sale, to find a solution, or to request help. Don't demand answers; instead, explain what you, your readers, and your organization need to reach that mutual goal.

1. TO DEMONSTRATE A SOLUTION. Present the challenge and then clearly demonstrate why your idea or point of view will provide a solution. Then clearly state the benefit — e.g., "With our current IT system, all of our offices operate independently. This fact slows our sales process by two to three days and increases our cost for customer care by about 30 percent. Please approve this new system to unify our systems, cut costs, and significantly improve customer service."

Challenge ⇨ Solution ⇨ Benefit

2. TO GET SUPPORT OR APPROVAL. Present the challenge, present the solution or benefit, and ask for support. Finish your message by writing, "I'd be happy to answer any questions, and I hope you can support our request for" something or some action.

Challenge ⇨ Solution or benefit ⇨ Ask for support

3. TO GET TO THE NEXT STEP. Present the challenge, clearly explain the current situation, and request help or support to get to the next step. Finish by writing, "Can we meet to discuss the next step?" or "We'd like your approval to move to Step 2 by the end of the quarter," or " What do you think is the next step? Please let me know."

Challenge ⇨ Current situation ⇨ Request to get to the next step

EXAMPLES OF KEY SENTENCES
WHEN YOU WRITE TO PERSUADE

4. TO REQUEST HELP. Present the current situation, clearly state the challenge, and ask for help to make a sale or resolve a problem that you face. To ask for help, write statements along these lines: "Can you please join us on this important sales call?" or "Can you suggest some different ways we might work more effectively with our Toronto office?"

Current situation   ⇨   Challenge you face   ⇨   Request for help

5. TO GET ADVICE. Present the challenge and clearly explain the sticking point. Then ask for further direction if it's important to get advice on what you should do next, where you can find information, or whom you should contact. Finish by asking questions along these lines: "Can you suggest what our next step should be?" or "Do you have an idea where we can go for more information or specific answers?"

Challenge   ⇨   Sticking point   ⇨   Request for advice

6. TO PROPOSE MORE WORK. Present a challenge you've already overcome, and then clearly explain the new solution and benefit that you or your team can provide. Write along these lines to pitch what you're ready to do: "The entire team has worked 12-hour days to complete Phase 4. With your approval of Phase 5, we'll continue to exemplify the company's 'Customer First' strategy as we complete the project."

Past challenge   ⇨   Request for approval   ⇨   Prediction of success

Writing to persuade can feel challenging, especially when you write to someone who has more seniority than you do. Try adapting these sentences to your writing needs the next time you need to send a persuasive message.

FILL IN STEP 3 FOR YOUR OWN DOCUMENT

Now you've reviewed the first three steps to take when you write: considering your readers' point of view, deciding what you want to accomplish, and stating your main point clearly in a key sentence.

Think of the document you need to write for your own work. Use the space below to write a key sentence that expresses your main message. When you're done, turn to page 56 and copy in the key sentence you decide on.

STEP 4:

LIST THE FACTS AND IDEAS THAT WILL
ACCOMPLISH YOUR PURPOSE.

When you start to write something, you usually have a general sense of what ideas you should include. But you still have to determine exactly what ideas readers need to hear before they're likely to feel fully persuaded or fully informed.

Start this step by writing down every idea that might persuade or inform your readers. The key is to give yourself permission to write down every idea that comes to mind when you ask yourself two basic questions:

> **WRITING TO PERSUADE:**
>
> *Why* should readers do what I want them to do?
> [e.g., why should they make a purchase?]
>
> **WRITING TO INFORM:**
>
> *What* do readers need to know?
> [e.g., what do they need to learn about a new procedure that will start in one week?]

At this brainstorming stage of the planning process, it's vital to write quickly without evaluating items on your list and blocking the flow of facts and ideas. That process comes in Step 5, when you decide which ideas you'll keep and which you'll throw out.

BRAINSTORM YOUR IDEAS TO SOLVE PROBLEMS

The brainstorming process is similar whether one person is planning Step 4 of a document, or a team is meeting to come up with creative solutions to a shared problem. The purpose of brainstorming is to free yourself to come up with as many ideas, questions, and answers as possible that fit a criterion you have in mind.

Allow yourself to generate facts and ideas without stopping the flow. Begin with a question such as, "Why should my reader do what I want?" or, "What does my reader need to know about this topic?" Write down every point that comes to mind without censoring, evaluating, or even organizing the points.

Don't worry about whether an idea will go into your final draft: just keep going until you believe you've written down everything that might be important to advance your document's purpose. You'll eliminate unnecessary or redundant ideas later.

You may get stuck. If so, then take a walk, tackle another task, or talk about the situation with a colleague. Then return to the brainstorming process.

Focus again on your starting questions about your reader. Read through your list, and add any additional ideas that come to mind. Then you'll be ready for the final step of document planning: organizing the ideas you'll send.

PRACTICE 1.4

Try the brainstorming process on the next three pages with a practice situation that reviews Steps 1–4.

Imagine that you're a car salesman replying to an email with a question from a young man and woman. They don't know much about cars, and they'd like to buy their first new car together.

You've met with them once, and you know that they care about fuel efficiency and want a car with an integrated hands-free phone device. You know that the young man injured his back and wants a car with a very comfortable front seat. You think one model at your dealership might be perfect for them. Their email gives you a chance to write back and tell them why.

Turn the page for Steps 1 through 3 of this practice.

PRACTICE 1.4, continued

STEP 1

1. Look at what you're going to write from your readers' point of view. In this case, imagine you're the salesman who's putting himself in his customers' shoes. Here's a list of questions you should consider before you write anything to them.

ARE YOUR READERS ...

❑ Expecting to hear from you?

❑ Familiar with the subject?

❑ Already interested in what you have to say?

❑ Likely to consider you an authority on the subject?

❑ Likely to find what you have to say useful?

❑ Familiar with your views on the subject?

❑ Already committed to a point of view?

❑ Likely to agree with your point of view?

❑ Likely to find your message uncomfortable?

Steps 2 and 3 of the Practice are on the next page.

PRACTICE 1.4, continued

STEPS 2–3

2. Decide what you want to accomplish:

    - **TO PERSUADE** the readers to buy the car, OR

    - **TO INFORM** the readers about the car's features

    In this situation, there is definitely something you want your readers to do. So your primary purpose is to persuade your readers.

3. Compose a key sentence that says exactly what you want the readers to do:

    I want my readers to _____

    _____ .

Hint   Your key sentence should clearly state what action you want your readers to do, e.g., "You should consider buying model _____ from our dealership."

Step 4 of the Practice is on the next page.

PRACTICE 1.4, continued

STEP 4

4. Now list the ideas that will accomplish your purpose.

    You're ready to collect information that will persuade your readers to buy the car from you — advancing your business needs as a salesman and theirs as consumers. Remember to keep your readers' point of view in mind, and look for points that will directly interest them.

    Which of the following facts and ideas are likely to be influential? Put an **X** beside each thought that might *not* sway the readers.

    ❏   "The model includes the hands-free phone link I remember they mentioned."

    ❏   "This model gets excellent mileage."

    ❏   "I want to sell more cars this month than Will sells."

    ❏   "This model's seats are unusually comfortable."

    ❏   "It's inside the price range they mentioned."

    ❏   "This is one of our more expensive models."

    ❏   "They'd be safer in this model than in the cars made by another company they mentioned when I met them."

    If you put an **X** beside "This is one of our more expensive models" and "I want to sell more cars this month than Will sells," then you're correct. Those two statements may be true, but the dealership's profit and the salesman's personal competitiveness won't persuade the potential buyers to do what he wants.

    It would be natural for both ideas to come up during brainstorming, but you wouldn't want to write them down since they don't advance your persuasive purpose.

FILL IN STEP 4 FOR YOUR OWN DOCUMENT

Now think back to the document you need to write for work. Use the space below to list facts and ideas that will advance your purpose. When you're done, turn to page 56 and copy in your final list.

STEP 5:

GROUP YOUR FACTS AND IDEAS INTO CATEGORIES.

Whenever you write anything longer than a few sentences, it's important to organize your ideas by grouping them into categories before you start writing. These categories provide the reader with a road map — a route through the information, and a way to break up the journey into phases.

For example, look at how people learn long-distance phone numbers in the US. Try learning this number:

5135553938

It's hard, isn't it? But the number is much easier to learn when it's broken down into groups:

AREA CODE	PREFIX	NUMBER
513	555	3938

(513) 555-3938 OR 513-555-3938 OR 513.555.3938

In the same way, you can help your readers understand what you have to say by grouping your ideas into related topics during your planning process.

Grouping your ideas also makes it easier to write the first draft, because you won't have to worry about where to begin paragraphs. As you'll see, each group of ideas forms one topic. In focused writing, one topic equals one paragraph or paragraph group — often under a heading if it's a long document section.

There is no standard way to organize ideas. It's a highly individual process that emerges from the situation and from your own unique insights into what different ideas have in common.

PRACTICE 1.4

Can you name a trait that the three items in each of these two groups have in common?

GROUP A	GROUP B
hammers	paper clips
nails	staples
paint	white-out

The answer is on the next page.

ANSWERS

GROUP A	GROUP B
hammers	paper clips
nails	staples
paint	white-out

You may have noted that the three items in Group A are supplies you could get in a hardware store while the three items in Group B are office supplies.

You could also regroup the items this way:

GROUP C	GROUP D
paint	hammers
white-out	nails
	paper clips
	staples

Now the two items in Group C are things you wouldn't want to spill, while the four items in Group D are solid objects.

GROUP IDEAS TO MANAGE A PROJECT

Grouping your ideas is a helpful process for many professional activities — e.g., **PROJECT MANAGEMENT.** Clear categories of ideas can give you an overview of all the project details you need to track and complete, grouped by deadlines and types of activity.

Grouping your project details into categories can help you manage complexity, stay on schedule, and not lose sight of the forest for the trees. And clear writing is often vital to keep your project management on track.

A grouping of ideas can become your organizational scheme for writing a document. Your scheme will depend mostly on what type of information you need to organize and what your writing purpose is.

An organizational scheme is more useful than a conventional outline (e.g., I, II.A, II.B, III, etc.) because it lets your information determine how you organize your document. With conventional outlines, many people tend to start with a category scheme *before* they know what information they'll include. That approach is like moving your family into a pre-furnished house when you have the opportunity to choose the blueprint and furnishings of a new, custom-built home.

Try not to force your ideas into a preset outline or an organizational scheme that doesn't feel like a good fit for your message. The next page shows three typical organizational schemes you can choose between:

- Organization by overarching topics
- Organization by chronological order
- Organization through comparison or contrast

1. **OVERARCHING TOPICS.** Suppose you're providing readers with details about three different software applications. You might group information about the applications into these three categories of overarching details — describing each topic for all three applications before moving to the next topic:

- Cost
- Ease of use
- Special features

2. **CHRONOLOGICAL ORDER.** Group information by chronology when you want to show events or actions that change over time. For instance, you might use either of these organizational schemes to present information about a long-term research project:

SCHEME 1:	SCHEME 2:
First year	Past history
Second year	Present status
Third year	Projection for the future

3. **COMPARISON AND CONTRAST.** Sometimes the most effective way to organize information is to break it up into two categories and compare them. You might use one of these schemes to give managers details to evaluate two locations that might be suitable for your company's new offices:

SCHEME 1:	Pros/cons
SCHEME 2:	Advantages/disadvantages
SCHEME 3:	Meets/fails to meet our criteria

In addition to these three organizational schemes, you could consider organizing your ideas by type of task, priority, or date needed. There is no right or wrong way to organize information; the important objective is to develop an organizational scheme that fits your ideas and will make sense to your readers.

PRACTICE 1.5

Here's a list of different foods. Imagine you're writing an event email about these foods, and organize them into two or three logical groups.

chocolate ice cream	sweet-and-sour pork
spaghetti	strawberries
hamburgers	artichokes
spare ribs	pecan pie
cheese Danish	roast turkey
crab	walnut torte

ANSWERS

Here are some ways to group the foods in the list above. You may have grouped them differently; it's only important that you found some logical organizational scheme.

CHRONOLOGICAL ORDER

MAIN COURSE OPTIONS

sweet-and-sour pork

spaghetti

roast turkey

hamburgers

spare ribs

crab

artichokes

DESSERT OPTIONS

chocolate ice cream

cheese Danish

pecan pie

walnut torte

strawberries

TOPICS

HIGH IN VITAMINS

strawberries

artichokes

HIGH IN PROTEIN

chocolate ice cream

hamburgers

spare ribs

crab

sweet-and-sour pork

roast turkey

HIGH IN STARCH

spaghetti

cheese Danish

pecan pie

walnut torte

COMPARISON AND CONTRAST (NAMELY, PROS AND CONS):

FOODS I LIKE

chocolate ice cream

cheese Danish

roast turkey

spare ribs

sweet-and-sour pork

strawberries

crab

FOODS I DISLIKE

hamburgers

pecan pie

artichokes

spaghetti

walnut torte

PRACTICE 1.6

Now suppose you're writing an online article about these athletic activities:

surfing	swimming	volleyball
skiing	scuba diving	baseball
wind surfing	football	mountain climbing
snowboarding	basketball	rock climbing
mountain biking	canoeing	kayaking
rollerblading	tennis	jogging

Here's one way you might organize them:

WATER-RELATED

surfing	basketball	rollerblading
canoeing	skiing	rock climbing
wind surfing	tennis	football
swimming	volleyball	jogging
scuba diving	baseball	snowboarding
kayaking	mountain climbing	
	mountain biking	

NOT WATER-RELATED

Now you try it. Organize the activities another way:

OMIT INFORMATION TO SOLVE A PROBLEM

Sometimes you have too much information for one document — say, an email that you need to be brief. Some ideas may not be important enough to send to your reader, even though these ideas fit into logical groups that you've identified.

Deciding what ideas to omit represents **PROBLEM SOLVING,** a core professional ability. One frequent business problem is deciding whether an idea is relevant, off-topic, or not important enough to include in your current message.

Successful professional communication is often the result of problem solving — from deciding what details do and don't belong in a report, to focusing the agenda for a presentation, to deciding just how much to say in a proposal.

Business readers rarely have time to spare, and overcrowding your message will waste their time. That's a significant problem. You'll successfully solve many communication challenges by identifying which ideas belong in your message, omitting the rest, and moving on.

ANSWERS

Here's one way you might have grouped the activities:

LITTLE OR NO COST	MODERATELY EXPENSIVE	EXPENSIVE
swimming	surfing	canoeing
football	tennis	skiing
basketball	mountain climbing	scuba diving
volleyball	rock climbing	mountain biking
baseball	rollerblading	wind surfing
jogging		snowboarding
		kayaking

Next, let's look at an example of how one writer might group ideas for an email to inform a group of readers.

USE TOPIC SENTENCES TO GROUP YOUR POINTS

Each category of information will usually form one paragraph when you write your first draft. Topic sentences are key sentences for the middle paragraphs of your text. They're signposts you can plant in your writing to show your readers the way forward through your sequence of ideas, from one category to the next.

Each topic sentence should introduce the paragraph's central topic, provide context to help readers follow your points, and indicate which points are most important.

Here's an example of a way to group ideas for an email to pass on information.

SITUATION:

Joan Huang is in charge of a conference called Newest Trends in Evaluating Performance. She wants everyone in her department to know what will be covered during the conference and to understand how to get there.

READERS:	Joan's staff
PURPOSE:	To inform
KEY SENTENCE:	"Here's how you can attend the upcoming Newest Trends in Evaluating Performance conference."

Joan asks herself, "What do my staff members need to know?" and she lists these questions:

- Where will it be held?

- What are the dates and times?

- What if I can't attend?

- How and where do I sign up?

- Who's responsible for travel and housing arrangements?

- Who's paying the airfare and hotel expenses?

QUESTIONS TO ANSWER

Next, Joan answers the questions:

- Where will it be held?
  – Marriott Hotel, San Francisco
  – Crown Room

- What are the dates and times?
  – February 14 and 15
  – 9 a.m.–5 p.m. each day
  – Complete agenda available a week before the conference, around Feb. 6th

- What if I can't attend?
  – Ask Josie at ext. 405 for presentation reports

- How and where do I sign up?
  – Josie has all the forms, and they're due January 31

- Who's responsible for travel and housing arrangements?
  – Sue at Whole Universe Travel

- Who's paying the airfare and hotel expenses?
  – The company

Joan groups the points into two categories. Then she writes a topic sentence for each category and puts them in order.

- **Logistics:** the conference is scheduled for February 14 and 15

- **Arrangements:** the company is paying all expenses; here's how to make arrangements and receive presentation reports if you cannot attend

COMPLETED EMAIL

TO: **Department Members**
FROM: **Joan Huang, Department Manager**
SUBJECT: **Annual conference**

Hello,

Here is the information you've been waiting for about the upcoming conference, Newest Trends in Evaluating Performance.

Logistics

The conference is scheduled for February 14 and 15. All events will take place in the Crown Room of the San Francisco Marriott between 9 a.m. and 5 p.m. A detailed agenda will be available the week of February 6.

Arrangements

The company is paying all expenses. Here's how to make arrangements or receive the presentation reports if you cannot attend:

- To sign up, call Josie at extension 405 for a registration form. Make sure you return the form to Josie by 5 p.m. on January 31.

- To make air and hotel reservations, call Sue at Whole Universe Travel at (510) 555-6477.

- If you cannot attend, ask Josie to put your name on the distribution list for presentation reports.

If you have any questions about this conference, call me at extension 263. I hope to see you at the conference in February.

Best,

Joan

APPLY WHAT YOU'VE LEARNED

FILL IN STEPS 1–4 FOR YOUR OWN DOCUMENT

READER:

PURPOSE:

KEY SENTENCE:

MAIN FACTS AND IDEAS:

APPLY WHAT YOU'VE LEARNED

FILL IN STEP 5 FOR YOUR OWN DOCUMENT

Now it's time to pull together the first four steps you filled out on page 56 for a document you're writing for your own work. Use the space below to group your ideas into categories that will help your reader understand your meaning.

When you've completed all five steps of the writing plan, you'll have a logical, effective structure to accomplish your specific business goals. It's going to be easy now to move from this plan to your first draft. You won't have to spend more time thinking about how to get started, what you want to say, or how you should organize your ideas. You've taken all those steps already by efficiently planning your document.

You can use the activity on page 166, at the end of Lesson 5, to turn your writing plan from Lesson 1 into a complete email. Pages 167 to 173 feature writing sheets you can also use to turn your writing plan from this lesson into a longer first draft.

LESSON 1 REVIEW

To review Lesson 1, write the correct ideas in the blanks below. The page numbers for each topic are listed in parentheses.

1. To begin a writing plan, think about what you're going to write from your

   _____ point of view (page 15).

2. Decide on your primary purpose: either to _____ or to

   _____ readers (22).

3. Compose a _____ that expresses your most

   important _____ (28).

4. To decide what information to include when you write, list the

   _____ and _____ that

   will accomplish your primary purpose (37).

5. If you're writing to persuade readers, ask "_____

   should readers do what I want them to do?" (37).

6. If you're writing to inform readers, ask "_____

   do readers need to know?" (37).

7. After listing the ideas to include in your writing, the next step is to

   _____ your facts and ideas into categories (44).

2   WRITE THE FIRST DRAFT

INTRODUCTION

Your first draft almost writes itself after you complete your writing plan. You've already done the hard work — identifying your purpose in writing, finding the right words to express your main message, and selecting and organizing the facts and ideas you need to persuade or inform your readers.

The next step is to use that plan to write a first draft that accomplishes your professional goals.

OBJECTIVES

In this lesson, you'll learn to write a professional and effective first draft with these steps:

- Review your writing plan and revise it as needed to make sure the plan is sound

- Write an opening that catches readers' attention and clearly states your topic

- Limit sentence and paragraph length to keep ideas easy to grasp

- Write a closing that sums up your ideas and clearly tells readers what happens next

WHAT YOU'LL NEED:

- The writing plan that you completed over the course of Lesson 1 (pages 56–57)
- Sample documents you've written for your job

REVIEW YOUR WRITING PLAN

Before you start the first draft, take a few moments to review your writing plan. There are two reasons:

- If there are any inconsistencies in your plan, it's important to correct them before you begin the first draft.

- Reviewing the plan helps you keep it fresh in your mind when you start writing. This review is important if time has passed since you finished the planning phase.

Here are some questions to ask as you review your writing plan:

❑ Have I considered my readers' point of view?

❑ Have I correctly identified my primary purpose in writing?

❑ Does my key sentence advance my primary purpose?

> **WRITING TO PERSUADE:**
>
> ❑ Explain why readers should do what I want them to do
>
> **WRITING TO INFORM:**
>
> ❑ Explain what readers need to know

❑ Have I included all the information my readers will need?

❑ Have I eliminated unnecessary information?

❑ Have I grouped the information logically and effectively — from the readers' point of view?

If you answer no to any of these questions, then take a closer look at your writing plan. Before you start the first draft, be sure your writing plan does two things:

- Highlights ideas that will accomplish your purpose in writing
- Helps your reader do business with you

Write an inviting opening

Why do you think the first part of a document is important? Write down a few reasons:

Many businesspeople are drowning in documents; you have to explain your message quickly and clearly to catch and keep your readers' attention. The opening lines of a document are often your only chance to hook your readers' attention: they may move on to another task if your opening is ambiguous or long-winded.

An effective opening covers these bases:

- Catches the readers' attention

- Establishes a personal contact with them and sets the right tone — two particularly important tasks when your primary purpose is to persuade

- Includes a key sentence that explains what you're writing about

- Presents a quick snapshot of your message in no more than three or four sentences

Read these two versions of the same opening. Which one makes you want to continue?

VERSION 1   This is in reference to your recent email, which was passed to this department for review. Unfortunately, the information you requested is not available at this point in time.

VERSION 2   Thank you for asking about the August 5 class. We don't yet know the location or the instructor's name, but we should be able to send you all the details by July 15.

Version 1 may not sound satisfying to you. It uses clichés such as "This is in reference to," and this empty language isn't likely to engage readers. As an opening, this version lacks specific information and leaves the reader with unanswered questions — how do departments communicate with one another, and will the information be available later on? If so, what's a likely date?

Version 2, in contrast, was clearly written by one person to another. It directly answers specific questions. The writer gets to the point quickly and provides useful details.

Here are some effective and problematic openings arranged in pairs. In each set, put an **X** next to the opening that you think best meets the criteria above.

  _____ **A:** We hereby acknowledge receiving your message dated April 20. Your complaint has been taken under advisement.

  _____ **B:** Thank you for telling us about the missing parts in the equipment you recently purchased. We will be happy to replace the parts, but we need the information listed below.

  _____ **A:** Per your recent inquiry concerning delivery of your car, a message was sent to the attention of the manufacturer. We are pleased to provide you with a copy of the response we received.

  _____ **B:** We are happy to say that your car will arrive on Wednesday, August 1. You can pick it up any time after noon on Thursday, August 2.

If you preferred Version B in each pair, then you recognized the more effective opening.

One way to improve openings is to avoid overused phrases such as these:

With reference to …	Regarding your recent communication …
Enclosed, please find …	We are in receipt of your message …
Please be advised …	On the above date and time …
Attached herewith …	This is in regards to …
I am writing to inform you …	Per your request …

Here are some examples of how to replace overused phrases with simple, direct language:

OVERUSED	SIMPLE AND DIRECT
Per your request for procedural instructions …	As you asked, here are the steps of the procedure you should follow.
Please be advised that your shipment has been delayed.	Unfortunately, your shipment has been delayed.
Enclosed, please find copies of your last three invoices.	I have enclosed copies of your last three invoices. I am attaching copies of your last three invoices. Here are copies of your last three invoices.
I am writing to inform you that your shipment has been located.	We have found your shipment.
This is in regards to your recent communication regarding our services.	Thank you for telling us that you appreciated our customer service team's response to your questions. Thank you for taking the time to tell us about your dissatisfaction with our customer service team's response to your questions.
We are in receipt of your message in regard to the vacant position.	As you asked, we are happy to send you an application for the position of Community Relations Director.

PRACTICE 2.1

Use your imagination to fill in missing details, and revise the three openings below so that they meet the following four goals:

- Catch the reader's attention
- Make a personal contact with the reader and set the right tone
- Include a key sentence that explains what you're writing about
- Keep the opening under three sentences long

OPENING 1

Please be advised that your comments on the proposed computer training program, received by this office on June 3, have been reviewed and, where appropriate, incorporated into the program.

_____

_____

_____

_____

_____

_____

OPENING 2

I am writing to inform you that payment has not yet been received for the current month. The conditions of your note specify that payment be made no later than the first day of each month. It is imperative that payment be received within 10 days of the date of this message.

_____

_____

_____

_____

_____

_____

_____

OPENING 3

Attached, please find a copy of the Assistant Director's message to Acme Products. Also attached is a copy of the message to Alex Stein from Acme's CEO, as well as a copy of the Test Plan form, which was written by Bill Jordan.

_____

_____

_____

ANSWERS

Here are the kinds of changes you might have made.

OPENING 1

ORIGINAL   Please be advised that your comments on the proposed computer training program, received by this office on June 3, have been reviewed and, where appropriate, incorporated into the program.

REVISION   Thank you for your comments on the proposed computer training program. We have incorporated the suggested changes listed below.

OPENING 2

ORIGINAL   I am writing to inform you that payment has not yet been received for the current month. The conditions of your loan specify that payment be made no later than the first day of each month. It is imperative that payment be received within 10 days of the date of this message.

REVISION   We have not yet received your loan payment, which was due on April 1. Please make sure we receive it no later than April 25.

OPENING 3

ORIGINAL   Attached please find a copy of the Assistant Director's message to Acme Products. Also attached is a copy of the message to Alex Stein from Acme's CEO, as well as a copy of the Test Plan form, which was written by Bill Jordan.

REVISION   I am enclosing copies of the following documents:
- The Assistant Director's message to Acme Products
- The Acme CEO's message to Alex Stein
- Bill Jordan's Test Plan form

ADD A SUMMARY TO A LONGER DOCUMENT

When you're writing a report, business plan, or proposal, consider including a **SUMMARY** for your reader. A summary explains a long document's contents. Some summaries are aimed at a group of readers who need only a snapshot of the contents and won't read the full document.

Summaries help people grasp your most important message along with the key facts and ideas you've included to inform or persuade your reader. It's a good idea to write the summary *after* you've developed your writing plan, topic sentences, and headings. These elements represent your document's most important information, and they can lay the framework for a concise summary.

Keep the following points in mind when you write summaries:

- Always state your most important message at the summary's beginning

- Put the summary at the beginning of the document

- Keep the summary short (between half a page and a full page is ideal; one-tenth of the entire document length is another guideline)

- Make sure that the summary covers all the main points, in the same order as they appear in the document that follows

- Focus on the most important ideas, and remember that readers will turn to the main document if they need more details

<u>**TRY IT:**</u>   Read through a long document that one or more people at your organization have written, or have referred to for their work. Write a summary for the document if it doesn't have one, or analyze the summary if one is included. Decide what essential information the summary should contain to give the reader a heads-up for all the document's most important points.

Limit sentence and paragraph length

Some sentences are too long to grasp easily in one reading. People often have to read sentences twice when they're longer than 30 words. A single-spaced, printed page divided into just two or three paragraphs also looks dense and intimidating.

As a general rule, frame each sentence to include just one or two thoughts, and keep each sentence between an average length of 18 and 25 words. When you use technical or unusual terms, drop the count to 15 to 18 words. Occasionally adding shorter and longer sentences can add rhythm to your document, but longer sentences should be especially clear.

Here's how to determine whether your sentences are too long:

- Count the total words in five consecutive sentences that look typical for your document. Include numbers and small words such as *a, the, to*, etc.

- Divide the total by five to determine your average sentence length.

EXAMPLE

> The Data Processing Group has failed to meet its schedules for the past six months, causing delays and confusion throughout the organization. (22) To remedy this situation, please make sure all team members follow the Data Processing Organizational Plan procedures to the letter. (20)
> The plan, which was distributed to all the teams in November, clearly establishes objectives and priorities for all department projects. (20) The procedures it contains explain each team member's responsibilities in detail. (11) The procedures also provide steps to take in the case of problems. (12)

Here are the word counts for those five sentences:

- Words per sentence: 22 + 20 + 20 + 11 + 12 = **85**

- Average words per sentence: 85 ÷ 5 = **17**

PRACTICE 2.2

Here's a technique to gauge how easy your sentences are to follow.

1. On your own time, look at a sample of your writing.

2. Count the number of words in five consecutive, typical sentences. (A word processor's Word Count feature can save time.)

3. Write down the number of words in each sentence:

   - **Sentence 1:**

   - **Sentence 2:**

   - **Sentence 3:**

   - **Sentence 4:**

   - **Sentence 5:**

4. Add the five numbers and record the total: _____ .

5. Divide the total by five and record that number: _____ .

6. If the average sentence is longer than 25 words, try to pay closer attention to your sentence lengths.

Here's an easy, two-step method to revise a long sentence:

1. List the ideas.

2. Write a series of separate sentences that contain only one or two of those ideas each.

PRACTICE 2.3

Revise this long sentence with the method listed above.

> I worked with a number of managers and supervisors to explore the challenges that surfaced during the change process — including concerns about their own limitations, a sense of loss as a result of change, the reconciliation of conflicting needs and priorities, and ways to preserve their senses of worth as everyone else seemed to be moving forward. (57)

_____

_____

_____

_____

_____

ANSWERS

Your two-step revision might look like this:

1. List the ideas:

   > I worked with managers and supervisors to explore challenges that resulted from the change process, including the following:
   >
   > - Concerns about their limitations
   >
   > - A sense of loss as a result of change
   >
   > - Concerns about conflicting needs and priorities
   >
   > - Ways to preserve their senses of self-worth

2. Write a series of separate sentences that contain only one or two of those ideas each:

   > I worked with a number of managers and supervisors to explore challenges that resulted from the change process. (18) Two of the major issues concerned feelings about their own limitations and their senses of loss as a result of change. (21) In addition, they wanted to reconcile their conflicting needs and priorities. (11) Finally, they worked to preserve their own senses of self-worth as everyone else seemed to be moving forward. (18)

Lesson 3 covers techniques to write effective lists. Either the new list or the new paragraph would be much easier to read than the 57-word sentence above.

PRACTICE 2.4

Turn this problematic 55-word sentence into several shorter sentences.

> I have enclosed a survey form that will allow you to give me feedback about the process used to set up the display booth that will help us learn whether our customers were satisfied with the arrangements and if they were not, we want to know what specific changes we should make for next year.

1. List the ideas:

   _____

   _____

   _____

   _____

2. Write a series of separate sentences that contain only one or two of those ideas each:

   _____

   _____

   _____

   _____

   _____

   _____

   _____

   _____

Once you've listed the ideas and written out separate sentences for them, your revisions should look something like this. Sentence word counts are noted in parentheses.

1. List the ideas:

    We need to revisit the display booth procedure: (8)

    - I have enclosed a survey form for you to give me feedback about the process to set it up. (19)

    - Your feedback will help us learn whether our customers were satisfied with the arrangements. (14)

    - If they were not satisfied, we want to know what specific changes we should make for next year. (18)

2. Write a series of separate sentences that contain only one or two of those ideas each:

    We need to revisit the display booth procedure. (8) I have enclosed a survey form for you to give me feedback about the process to set it up. (19) Your feedback will help us learn whether our customers were satisfied with the arrangements. (14) If they were not satisfied, we want to know what specific changes we should make for next year. (18)

PRACTICE 2.5

Review your own writing and look for a sentence that's more than 24 words long. If you find one, write out the original here or on some note paper, and then revise it. If you don't find any sentences that long, skip to the next section of this lesson.

ORIGINAL:

_____

_____

_____

_____

_____

_____

REVISION:

_____

_____

_____

_____

_____

Use headings

Name two reasons to use headings in professional documents:

- _____

- _____

Here are some of the reasons you may have listed:

- Headings make it easier for people to find information

- Headings make a document look more attractive

- Headings are a good way to break up dense text

- Headings require you to group relevant ideas together, and this focused writing is easier for readers to follow

Headings make your documents easier to understand by presenting your reader with concise themes. Headings are especially useful when your document is long or complicated, or if it presents dense technical information.

The planning process itself helps you come up with the headings: once you group information into categories, your headings practically identify themselves.

Here's a single email without headings.

WITHOUT HEADINGS:

> Ali:
>
> Hope you can come to the annual Presidents' Circle Sales Meeting this summer. The meeting will be held at the Hilton in San Francisco and you should bring your updated presentations and spreadsheets. You can make travel arrangements yourself or Pam can help you. We'll have one day of learning with workshop leaders including Jamie Hartwell, Linda Lou, and Peter Panino, and one day to look internally at our processes with Jack Deiner.
>
> We're going to Alcatraz. It will be three days long with an optional dinner on Tuesday night. Sally is no longer available to help with travel arrangements. Another agenda will be sent out. You can come on Wednesday morning or Tuesday night but make sure that you're there till Friday morning. Bring comfortable walking shoes. If you make the travel arrangements yourself, use billing code 55789. You don't need to bring anything else. You were selected because you did a great job.

The next page shows the same email reorganized under a series of headings. The text takes up more space, but it's much easier to follow.

WITH HEADINGS:

Ali:

Because of the great job you did this year, you've been invited to the Presidents' Circle Sales Meeting in San Francisco this summer. Following is all the information you'll need to make your travel arrangements. We'll send you a more detailed agenda by May 1.

Meeting dates and location

The meeting will be held in the San Francisco Hilton from Tuesday, July 14th, through Friday, July 17th, 2013.

Travel arrangements

The travel process has changed, and Sally is no longer available to help. You can make arrangements yourself using your company credit card and billing code 55789, or ask Pam to help.

What to bring

Please bring your updated spreadsheets and presentations. Also, bring comfortable walking shoes for an outing to Alcatraz on Friday morning. We'll provide everything else you need.

Agenda

- Tuesday: meet for dinner at the hotel restaurant at 7 p.m. (optional)
- Wednesday: meetings 9–5 with Jamie Hartwell, Linda Lou, and Peter Panino, followed by dinner at Aziza
- Thursday: meetings 9–5 with Jack Deiner followed by dinner at La Mar Cebicheria
- Friday: morning excursion to Alcatraz; meeting convenes at 1 p.m.

I'll send out a detailed agenda by May 1; please let me know if you have any questions. We hope you're proud of all your successful work this year!

Notice that the revision above moves from general to specific information: from the name and purpose of the meeting to its date and location, to the steps necessary to get there, to the smaller details of a four-day agenda. The model below demonstrates how you can apply this clear organizational logic to your own documents.

THE JOURNALISTIC TRIANGLE

Have you ever noticed that the first paragraphs of many news articles contain the most important information? The rest of the article then provides details that support, explain, expand on, or illustrate that information.

News editors know that people often scan only the headline and first part of an article. That's why they often answer their readers' most important question right at the beginning, as shown in the example below.

Putting the most important information first answers the readers' most important question right away and provides a context for the details that follow.

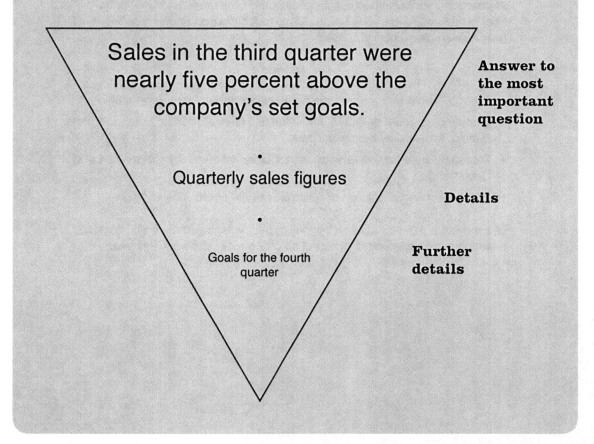

PRACTICE 2.6

Add headings to the paragraph below to make its topics more clear.

> Be prepared for adverse weather. In high winds, remove affected crews to shelter (inside the building or in a crawl space, etc.). Secure material from blowing off of structures, which can injure employees. Do not operate cranes in constant 30 MPH winds. Secure tower cranes when they are not in use and make allowances to prevent crane booms from clashing. Evacuate to the structure during a tornado if you are in trailer offices. Do not work outside during a lightning storm. Ensure that all in-place storm drain lines and receivers are operational.

_____

_____

_____

_____

_____

_____

_____

_____

_____

_____

_____

_____

_____

_____

_____

_____

_____

_____

ANSWERS

Here's one way to add headings to that paragraph.

Be prepared for the following kinds of bad weather:

High winds

- Remove affected crews to shelter (inside the building or in a crawl space, etc.)

- Secure material from blowing off of structures, which can injure employees

- Do not operate cranes in constant 30 MPH winds

- Secure tower cranes when they are not in use and make allowances to prevent crane booms from clashing

Tornados and lightning

- Evacuate to the structure during a tornado if you are in trailer offices

- Do not work outside during a lightning storm

COUNT IDEAS FOR A USER-FRIENDLY DOCUMENT

Any business document is more likely to hold readers' attention when it displays **ANALYTICAL SKILLS.** Analysis is a natural part of the planning process as you examine your ideas to see how they relate to one another. Quantitative (numeric) analysis can be simple: just write out your ideas, count them, and then include numbers in your sentences and headings.

Numbers can act as a heads-up for information that a reader is about to encounter. For instance, you might begin a bulleted list with the introductory statement, "We see <u>four</u> primary benefits: • • •." Or you might add a section heading that reads, "<u>Four</u> Benefits," followed by four paragraphs — one for each benefit as you explain it to the reader.

(By the way, it's much easier to read information under numbered headings or in a list than as words such as "First …. Second …. Fourth" across one or more paragraphs. Headings or a list prevent the reader from skimming past a number and losing track of your logic.)

Clearly quantifying your information helps give the impression that you thoroughly understand your topic. It also shows that you've taken some extra effort to help your readers understand it, too.

<u>TRY IT:</u>   Look through some documents you've written for your job — especially documents that seemed especially complex at the time. Could simple quantitative analysis have helped your readers grasp your ideas more easily?

Write effective closing paragraphs

A strong closing achieves the following goals:

- Makes a final personal contact with readers (a crucial factor when you're writing to persuade)

- Wraps up any loose ends

- Tells readers clearly what happens next

- Uses specific language

A closing paragraph might also advance your purpose in these ways:

- By restating what readers should do

- By restating what readers should know

Compare these two closings. Which do you prefer?

CLOSING 1: It would be appreciated if this situation could be rectified in a timely manner. Any questions can be addressed to this writer at the number above.

CLOSING 2: Please find the missing file by June 15. If I can help in any way, please call me at (510) 555-6477.

You probably preferred Closing 2. The first closing is impersonal and vague. The second is specific to the situation and conveys useful information.

Here are some impersonal, vague closings to avoid:

Please contact the above regarding time constraints on the aforementioned policy.

Your assistance and cooperation will be greatly appreciated.

Do not hesitate to contact this writer should you require additional information.

Minor changes can transform those closings by making them specific to one piece of writing:

INSTEAD OF ...	TRY THIS ...
Please contact the above regarding time constraints on the aforementioned policy.	Please call John Alcotts about this policy's expiration date.
Your assistance and cooperation will be greatly appreciated.	I will be grateful for any help you can give me in tracking down the correct phone number.
Do not hesitate to contact this writer should you require additional information.	If you need a map or more detailed directions, please let me know.

PRACTICE 2.7

Write a closing for this message.

> Dear Mr. Hogan:
>
> Thank you for asking about our new Flexible Loan Program. I'm happy to send a brochure that describes the program and includes an application.
>
> We designed this program after many discussions with customers about what types of lending arrangements they wanted. I think you'll find it offers some unique ways to meet your financial needs.

_____

_____

_____

_____

_____

_____

ANSWERS

The last paragraph below is one possible conclusion for the message.

> Dear Mr. Hogan:
>
> Thank you for asking about our new Flexible Loan Program. I'm happy to send a brochure that describes the program and includes an application.
>
> We designed this program after many discussions with customers about what types of lending arrangements they wanted. I think you'll find it offers some unique ways to meet your financial needs.
>
> Please let me know if you have any questions. If I haven't heard from you, I'll call in two weeks to see if you'd like to apply for a loan under this new program.

**WRITE THE FIRST DRAFT
OF THE DOCUMENT YOU PLANNED IN LESSON 1**

You may have used Lesson 1 to plan an email. If so, you can use the activity on page 166, at the end of Lesson 5, to turn your plan into a complete draft with an effective opening, good sentence flow, and an effective closing. If you planned another kind of document in Lesson 1, pages 167 to 173 feature writing sheets you can use to turn your writing plan into a longer first draft, with or without headings.

LESSON 2 REVIEW

Fill in the blanks with the correct word or phrase. The page numbers for each topic are listed in parentheses.

1. Before you start a first draft, always take a few moments to

    _____ (page 60).

2. An effective opening covers these bases (61):

    - Catches the readers' _____

    - Establishes a _____ contact with them and sets the right tone

    - Includes a _____ that explains what you're writing about

    - Presents a quick snapshot of your message in no more than _____

      _____

3. Headings make it easier for people to _____ and also make a document _____ (75).

4. A strong closing achieves the following goals (82):

    - Makes a final _____ with readers

    - Wraps up any _____

    - Tells readers clearly what _____

    - Uses _____ language

3   USE CONCISE LANGUAGE

> "I didn't have time to write a short letter, so I wrote a long one instead."
>
> — Mark Twain

INTRODUCTION

Unnecessary words are obstacles to good business writing. They clutter up your sentences and slow your readers down, and they can also make your documents boring. By eliminating unnecessary words, you can keep your readers' interest and make your writing easier to follow.

OBJECTIVES

In this lesson, you'll learn to write more professionally and effectively with these strategies:

- Finding single words for one-word ideas
- Avoiding repetition
- Eliminating wasteful verbs and clauses
- Using lists to present ideas logically and concisely

You'll need some sample documents that you've written for work to complete some activities in this lesson.

Here are a few examples of sentences with clutter — words that take up space without adding meaning. Which words do you think are unnecessary?

- Please let me know as to whether you will attend the party.

- The noise level of the trains arriving and departing from the station is low by the current standards of the rapid-transit industry.

- There are several employees who want to take vacations in June.

Here are some words that it would be better to eliminate:

- Please let me know ~~as to~~ whether you will attend the party.

- The noise level of the arriving and departing ᴧ trains ~~from the station~~ is low by ~~the~~ current standards. ~~of the rapid-transit industry.~~

- ~~There are several~~ ᴧ Several employees ~~who~~ want to take vacations in June.

In this lesson, you'll practice revising long-winded sentences. Then you'll review your own writing to see if you can make it more concise.

Use one word for a one-word idea

Sometimes you can collapse several words or a long phrase into one word that conveys your message quickly and clearly: for instance, *at a time prior to* simply means "before." The longer phrase is dull and bulky. The single word does the same job more efficiently.

At other times, you can collapse a multiword phrase into one word by identifying the most important word of the phrase, turning that word into a different part of speech, and cutting out words that don't enhance your meaning.

ORIGINAL:	We are in agreement with you about the contract terms.
REVISION:	We <u>agree</u> with you about the contract terms.

ORIGINAL:	She solved the problem in a clever way.
REVISIONS:	She solved the problem <u>cleverly</u>.
	She <u>cleverly</u> solved the problem.

In the first example, the short verb "agree" delivers the full meaning of the longer phrase "are in agreement."

In the second example, "clever" is the most important word in the phrase "in a clever way." The single word "cleverly" delivers the same meaning faster.

PRACTICE 3.1

Below or on some note paper, eliminate unnecessary words or revise the sentences to make them more concise.

ORIGINAL: The client visited the site of the project in May.

REVISION: The client visited <u>the project site</u> in May.

1. She drove in a reckless manner.

    _____

    _____

2. We conducted a survey of the members.

    _____

    _____

3. The manager made an offer to buy everyone coffee.

    _____

    _____

4. I believe this procedure will make an improvement in the way that reports are filed.

    _____

    _____

5. He called us in regard to his recent insurance claim.

    _____

    _____

6. Due to the fact that she was late filing the papers, our missed deadline is her responsibility.

    _____

    _____

ANSWERS

Your answers should look something like this:

1. She drove <u>recklessly</u>.

2. We <u>surveyed</u> the members.

3. The manager <u>offered</u> to buy everyone coffee.

4. I believe this procedure will <u>improve how</u> reports are filed.

5. He called us <u>about</u> his recent insurance claim.

6. She was late filing the papers and is <u>therefore</u> <u>responsible for</u> our missed deadline.

Avoid repetition

Business writers often use two or more words that mean exactly the same thing, making sentences unnecessarily wordy. Here are some common repetitive phrases:

alternative choices	important essentials
basic fundamentals	end result
serious crisis	future plans
final outcome	separate entities
past experience	advance warning
surrounding circumstances	two halves
equally as effective as	regular weekly meetings
symptoms indicative of	absolutely complete
desirable benefits	10 a.m. in the morning

These unnecessary words waste your readers' time. After all, a crisis is always serious, plans are always for the future, and 10 a.m. never happens at night!

PRACTICE 3.2

Eliminate the unnecessary repetitions in these sentences.

1. The urban residents of the city are unhappy with the new regulations.

    _____

    _____

2. The subterranean garage, located underground, is more secure than the old one.

    _____

    _____

3. Until last week, our group had the best record to date.

    _____

    _____

ANSWERS

Your revisions should look something like these. The underlined words convey the original sentences' full meaning without the unnecessary words you saw on the last page.

1. The <u>urban</u> residents are unhappy with the new regulations.

    — OR —

    The <u>city</u> residents are unhappy with the new regulations.

2. The <u>subterranean</u> garage is more secure than the old one.

3. <u>Until last week</u>, our group had the best record.

Eliminate wasteful possessives, clauses, and *there is* phrases

Some possessive word forms add nothing to a sentence but unnecessary length.

ORIGINAL:	<u>Their assumption is</u> that the company should always come first.
REVISION:	<u>They assume</u> that the company should always come first.

Some sentences can be streamlined by removing unnecessary *who*, *that*, and *which* clauses.

ORIGINAL:	The broker <u>who works in</u> Chicago sent the file <u>that is</u> incomplete to the home office.
REVISION:	The <u>Chicago</u> broker sent the <u>incomplete</u> file to the home office.

Phrases such as *there is, there are,* and *there may be* can also clutter up sentences — either on their own or by requiring extra words after the phrase.

ORIGINAL:	<u>There is</u> a new package on your desk.
REVISION:	A new package <u>is</u> on your desk.
ORIGINAL:	<u>There may be</u> several applicants who have the necessary background for this position.
REVISION:	Several applicants <u>may</u> have the necessary background for this position.

PRACTICE 3.3

Revise these sentences to make them more concise.

1. The members of the group who are interested in learning more about this software are welcome to attend the demonstration that will be conducted on February 16.

_____

_____

_____

2. Tomorrow's meeting, which will be held as always on the fourth floor, will include a speech about literacy in the workplace.

_____

_____

_____

3. There are thousands of hours wasted because no one can use the files that are out of date.

_____

_____

_____

ANSWERS

Your revisions should be similar to these:

1. **The members of the group who are interested in learning more about this software are welcome to attend the demonstration that will be conducted on February 16.**

    Group members interested in learning more about this software are welcome to attend the February 16 demonstration.

2. **Tomorrow's meeting, which will be held as always on the fourth floor, will include a speech about literacy in the workplace.**

    Tomorrow's fourth-floor meeting will include a speech about literacy in the workplace.

3. **There are thousands of hours wasted because no one can use the files that are out of date.**

    Thousands of hours are wasted because no one can use the out-of-date files.

PRACTICE 3.4

Here's a chance to pull together what you've learned so far. These sentences contain several kinds of clutter. Revise them to be more concise.

1. On the basis of your recent letter, I would like to take this opportunity to inform you that I will investigate the problem about the delay in processing your loan that you mentioned and send you a letter in order to report my findings.

2. At this point in time, it is our understanding that the new computer system will have the capability of processing 50 percent more information than the amount that is processed by our present system.

3. With regard to the current status of your request for additional office equipment, we have submitted a request for the purpose of obtaining the funds that are needed to initiate the purchase.

Check your answers on the next page.

ANSWERS

Your revisions should look something like these:

1. **On the basis of your recent letter, I would like to take this opportunity to inform you that I will investigate the problem about the delay in processing your loan that you mentioned and send you a letter in order to report my findings.**

   I will investigate the delay in processing your loan and write you with my findings.

2. **At this point in time, it is our understanding that the new computer system will have the capability of processing 50 percent more information than the amount that is processed by our present system.**

   We believe the new computer system will be able to process 50 percent more information than our present system can.

4. **With regard to the current status of your request for additional office equipment, we have submitted a request for the purpose of obtaining the funds that are needed to initiate the purchase.**

   We have requested funds to purchase the additional office equipment you requested.

PRACTICE 3.5

Revise the following three paragraphs to be as concise as possible without changing the meaning. Cross out or write in words without recopying the text. Some revisions are on the next page.

During the month of March, the people who are working on the HUF project team made a study of the past history of HUF in order to come to some conclusions as to whether the necessary information was available for the purpose of their determining the project goals.

•

The people who were members of this study team are of the opinion that the original analysis was done in an overly hasty manner and that there were several errors in the original conclusions. At this point in time, it appears that the main question is a matter of making a decision as to whether you should discontinue the project, or whether the team should undertake and perform a new analysis.

•

We have enclosed for your information the details that resulted from the study. Due to the fact that the short amount of time is a factor in this situation, we would greatly appreciate your reviewing the information, and we would appreciate your reaching a decision and informing us of it, in a prompt way.

ANSWERS

Your revisions should look something like this.

In March, the HUF project team studied HUF's history to decide whether they had enough information to determine the project goals.

•

The study team members believe that the original analysis was performed too hastily and that the conclusions included several errors. It now appears that the main question is whether you should discontinue the project or whether the team should undertake a new analysis.

•

We have enclosed the study results. Since time is short, we would greatly appreciate your reviewing the information promptly and telling us what you decide.

APPLY WHAT YOU'VE LEARNED

Read through one or more of your writing samples. If you find any sentences that look cluttered, select two or three and write them below. Then revise the sentences to be more concise.

ORIGINAL

_____

_____

_____

_____

REVISION

_____

_____

_____

_____

ORIGINAL

_____

_____

_____

_____

REVISION

_____

_____

_____

_____

ORIGINAL

_____

_____

_____

_____

REVISION

_____

_____

_____

_____

Use lists

How do you read business documents? You probably don't linger over the words the way you'd savor the prose of an amazing novel. Instead, you probably scan the document in a neutral frame of mind to see if its main points and details fit your needs as an employee, manager, client, or consumer.

When you consider your reader's point of view, it's easy to see that paragraphs are not always the best way to present information. The more technical or complicated information is, the more difficult it is to absorb in paragraph form.

Your goal as a business writer is to help readers find information as quickly as possible. To show consideration and speed things up for your reader, look for opportunities to present information in lists.

Read and compare the two messages on the next two pages. The first message is in paragraph form, and it's followed by a list-based revision. Both messages present the same information, but notice how much easier this information is to scan when it's in list form.

IN PARAGRAPH FORM

Dear Ms. Fratelli:

To process your loan application, we need the following information and documents as soon as possible.

The purpose of the loan should be entered in Item 3, along with the amount requested. List the balances on your bank accounts in Item 4A. Include the name and address of the institution and the account number. Use Items 4B, C, and D for certificates of deposit, stocks, etc., as shown.

The name and address of your previous employers should be entered in Item 6C if you have been at your current job for less than two years. Include an explanation of any gap in employment during the past ten years.

In Item 12A, please enter the name and address of the lender who holds your second deed of trust. The current balances on all your credit cards and outstanding loans should be entered in Items 16B and 16C, except for your automobile loans (Item 16D).

Finally, be sure to sign and date the form in Item 23.

The completed form should be sent to the loan processor along with copies of your last two years' tax returns and copies of your most recent pay stubs.

Please let me know if you have questions.

Sincerely,

Turn the page to see this information in list form.

AS TWO LISTS

Dear Ms. Fratelli:

To process your loan, we need a completed application as soon as possible. Please send the completed form to the loan processor along with copies of the following two documents:

- Your last two years' tax returns
- Your most recent pay stubs

On the application form, please complete the following items:

- Describe the purpose of the loan and enter the amount requested.
- List the balances on your bank accounts (Item 4A). Enter the name and address of the institution and the account number. List any certificates of deposit, stocks, etc., as shown (4B, 4C, and 4D).
- If you have been at your current job for less than two years, enter the name and address of your previous employers (6C). Include an explanation of any gap in employment during the past ten years.
- Enter the name and address of the lender who holds your second deed of trust (12A).
- List the current balances on all your credit cards (16B), outstanding loans (16C), and automobile loans (16D).
- Sign and date the form (Item 23).

Please let me know if you have questions.

Sincerely,

Leslie Tan

Follow these five list guidelines

You can use a list in business writing — and, often, you should use a list — whenever you present three or more related pieces of information. Lists are more effective than long paragraphs because they do three things:

- Communicate information quickly
- Save valuable writing time
- Reduce the chance of grammar and punctuation errors

To make sure your lists are easy to read, follow the five guidelines below. Full illustrations of each guideline follow this list.

1. **INTRODUCE THE LIST.** Every list needs an introductory statement, if only a few words, that identifies the list's theme and puts its items in context. Try to leave blank space between the introductory statement and the first list item.

2. **MAKE SURE THAT ALL ITEMS BELONG ON THE LIST.** All items on the list should relate directly to the introductory statement's unifying theme.

3. **BE CONSISTENT WITH INITIAL CAPITALIZATION, SENTENCE STRUCTURE, AND END PUNCTUATION:**

   - If you capitalize the first word of one line, capitalize the first word in every line.

   - Items in any single list should all be complete sentences or all be sentence fragments. List items that are sentence fragments should not end in periods, and they do not have to begin with capital letters (unless the first word is a proper noun).

   - For lists of complete sentences, end punctuation (periods or question marks) is only necessary for each item if any one item contains more than one sentence. (This list item contains three complete sentences.) In any list of complete sentences, you must use end punctuation after all the list's items if even one list item has end punctuation.

4. **KEEP THE LIST PARALLEL IN FORM.** For example, if one item begins with an *-ing* word, then all items should begin with *-ing* words.

5. **ORGANIZE THE LIST FOR YOUR READERS.** Lists that include more than five or six items can be hard to follow. Make lists easier to read by organizing the items into main points and subpoints (for instance, as Guideline 3 is divided into three smaller points above).

The next pages include full illustrations of each of these five guidelines.

Here are examples to illustrate the five guidelines for lists that you just read.

1. **INTRODUCE THE LIST.**

   A list should never stand alone: it needs an introductory statement. The first item in a list can't introduce the list itself.

   ### WITHOUT AN INTRODUCTION

   - <u>We offer several thank-you gifts</u>

   - A 10% discount on purchases during May

   - A discount coupon for the Milano Ristorante

   - A complimentary bottle of our best olive oil

   ### WITH AN INTRODUCTION

   <u>To express our appreciation for your business, we would like to offer you a choice of the following thank-you gifts:</u>

   - A 10% discount on purchases during May

   - A discount coupon for the Milano Ristorante

   - A complimentary bottle of our best olive oil

2. **MAKE SURE THAT ALL ITEMS BELONG ON THE LIST.** All items on the list should relate directly to the introductory statement's unifying theme.

   ### NOT ALL ITEMS RELATE TO THE INTRODUCTORY STATEMENT

   To prepare the conference room for training, please do the following:

   - Set up the tables in a U shape

   - Put two flipcharts in the front of the classroom

   - Place the projector on the table in the corner

   - <u>Design the training to include lots of exercises and opportunities for participants to practice</u>

ALL ITEMS RELATE TO THE INTRODUCTORY STATEMENT

To prepare yourself to deliver the training, make sure there will be lots of exercises and opportunities for participants to practice. <u>To prepare the conference room for the training, please do the following:</u>

- Set up the tables in a U shape

- Put two flipcharts in the front of the classroom

- Place the projector on the table in the corner

3. **BE CONSISTENT WITH INITIAL CAPITALIZATION, SENTENCE STRUCTURE, AND END PUNCTUATION.** Use end punctuation only when at least one item contains more than one complete sentence. If you use end punctuation for even one item, then you must use it for all items.

In paragraphs, sentences' periods and question marks tell readers when one sentence stops and another starts. In lists, end punctuation is only necessary if any one item contains more than one sentence because lists clearly show where one item stops and another begins.

END PUNCTUATION UNNECESSARY

We are unable to meet the original deadline for the following reasons:

- Two team members resigned in October and we have been unable to replace them

- The client expanded the project scope

- Three weeks of heavy rain made it impossible to complete our investigation

END PUNCTUATION NECESSARY

Here is a summary of our findings:

- The costs of moving to a new location will be higher than we originally <u>estimated.</u>

- According to the most current figures, the total cost will exceed <u>$150,000.</u>

- If we delay the move for five years, we will need an additional 10,000 square feet of <u>space.</u>

- Only 30 percent of our employees say they would be willing to move out of <u>California. Over</u> 60 percent, however, would be willing to consider a move to the <u>Bay Area.</u>

The following list is hard to read because its format is inconsistent.

INCONSISTENT

> We are unable to meet the original deadline for the following reasons:
>
> - Two team members resigned in October. We have been unable to replace them.
>
> - expanded project scope
>
> - Three weeks of heavy rain made it impossible to complete our investigation

The periods in the first item are inconsistent with the third item's lack of a period. The second item's uncapitalized sentence fragment is distracting because its form is inconsistent with the other two items. As a general rule, start list items with capital letters to make it easier to see where each item begins.

Here's the same list in a consistent format featuring complete sentences and no end punctuation.

CONSISTENT

> We are unable to meet the original deadline for the following reasons:
>
> - Two team members resigned in October and we have been unable to replace them
>
> - The client expanded the project scope
>
> - Three weeks of heavy rain made it impossible to complete our investigation

4. **KEEP THE LIST PARALLEL IN FORM.**

The items in a list must be parallel — presented in the same forms. For example, if one item begins with a verb, then all the list items must begin with verbs. If one item is a complete sentence, then all the items must be complete sentences.

NOT PARALLEL

The agenda for the March meeting includes the following:

- <u>Discussion of</u> the new health plan, which will be available to all permanent full-time employees

- <u>Whether</u> to revise the procedures manual

- <u>Early-retirement</u> policy

PARALLEL

At the March meeting, we will do the following:

- <u>Discuss</u> the new health plan, which will be available to all permanent full-time employees

- <u>Decide</u> whether to revise the procedures manual

- <u>Draft</u> an early-retirement policy

5. **ORGANIZE THE LIST FOR YOUR READERS.**

As a general rule, keep lists short. There should be no more than five or six items per list. When long lists are necessary, reorganize them as two or more shorter lists. Make long lists easier for your readers to scan by organizing the items into main points and subpoints.

TOO MANY ITEMS

Please supply the following for the conference that begins on October 22:

- 30 writing tablets for each meeting room
- Five desks with landlines in the community room
- An overhead projector for each meeting room
- Coffee, tea, and pastry in the foyer each morning
- Four round tables for each meeting room
- A basket of fruit for each table in the meeting rooms
- A registration table in the foyer

A revised list is on the next page.

ITEMS ORGANIZED WITH SUBPOINTS

Please supply the following items for the conference that begins on October 22. Please supply the following in each meeting room:

- 30 writing tablets

- An overhead projector

- Four round tables

- A basket of fruit for each table

Please supply five desks with landlines in the community room, and please supply the following in the foyer:

- Coffee, tea, and pastry each morning

- A registration table

USE LISTS AS A TEAM MEMBER OR LEADER

Lists have a wide variety of professional applications, whether you're composing a document as the leader of a company or as a member of a small team — e.g.,

- Setting out a variety of tasks or goals for a strategic plan

- Breaking down intricate processes into tidy, chronological steps

- Breaking down complex projects into clean phases with specific deadlines

- Identifying which tasks are completed and which tasks remain

- Itemizing a budget and allocating resources for different items

Lists aren't just for word processor documents. Look for ways to include lists in emails and other short professional documents in addition to longer letters, reports, proposals, and procedures. Whether you're a vice president, manager, team leader, or new hire, list formatting makes it easy for readers to literally follow your ideas.

PRACTICE 3.6

Use the space below or a blank sheet of paper to rewrite this paragraph in list format. Remember to include an introductory statement that tells readers what the list is about and establishes the context.

> The task force found that the customer service representatives need training in how to respond to problems and complaints. There is widespread unhappiness about the quality of food in the cafeteria, indicating the need to find another vendor. How to implement flexible hours without creating logistical problems requires additional study. Finally, field representatives need newer tablets, which have not been included in this year's budget. These are the primary areas of concern the members of the task force believe they need to address during the next six months.

_____

_____

_____

_____

_____

_____

_____

_____

_____

_____

_____

_____

_____

_____

_____

_____

Here are two ways to revise that paragraph into a list:

REVISION 1

> Below are the primary areas of concern the members of the task force believe they need to address during the next six months:
>
> - The customer service representatives need training in how to respond to problems and complaints
>
> - There is widespread unhappiness about the quality of food in the cafeteria, indicating the need to find another vendor
>
> - Additional study is needed to determine how to implement flexible hours without creating logistical problems
>
> - Field representatives need newer tablets, which have not been included in this year's budget

REVISION 2

> The task force members believe they must do the following during the next six months:
>
> - Train customer service representatives to respond to problems and complaints
>
> - Search for a new vendor to improve the cafeteria food's quality
>
> - Study ways to implement flexible hours without creating logistical problems
>
> - Find funds to provide field representatives with the newer tablets they need

PRACTICE 3.7

Use the space below or a blank sheet of paper to rewrite and reformat this paragraph as a list.

> To help us update our database, please review the enclosed listings and notify us of any changes. First, proofread each listing and indicate any necessary corrections. Then please enter the best contact information for clients to use, and at the same time verify that your telephone numbers and email addresses are correct. Finally, if you wish, you may add a maximum of two lines of explanation to each listing.

_____

_____

_____

_____

_____

_____

_____

_____

_____

_____

_____

_____

_____

_____

_____

_____

_____

ANSWERS

Here's one way to present the information more effectively. Your version might differ.

> To help us update our database, please review the enclosed listings and notify us of any changes:
>
> - Proofread each listing and indicate any necessary corrections
>
> - Enter the best contact information for clients to use
>
> - Verify that your telephone numbers and email addresses are correct
>
> - If you wish, add up to two lines of explanation to each listing

LESSON 3 REVIEW

Answer these questions to review what you've learned in this lesson. The page numbers for each topic are listed in parentheses.

1. _____ words are obstacles to good business writing. They clutter up your sentences and slow your readers down (page 87).

2. Sometimes you can collapse several words or a long phrase into _____ that conveys your message quickly and clearly (89).

3. You can streamline some sentences by removing wasteful _____ , _____, and _____ _____ phrases (93).

4. Try to break up lists that are longer than _____ or _____ items (110).

4

USE CLEAR LANGUAGE

INTRODUCTION

Language should convey your message swiftly and accurately. Some writers try to impress their readers with unnecessarily complex language, which slows down and confuses readers more often than it impresses them.

Unnecessarily complex language can result in miscommunication, frustration, and wasted time. The most effective and impressive writing makes complex ideas seem simple and clear. Simplicity and clarity are qualities that busy readers will value as they plow through accumulated messages in an email inbox or a pile of mail on their desks.

OBJECTIVES

In this lesson, you'll learn to write more professionally and effectively with these techniques:

- Using active language
- Using specific language
- Using plain English
- Avoiding jargon

You'll need some sample documents that you've written for work to complete some activities in this lesson.

Read through the following email. Its language is vague, pompous, and passive — making it hard to tell what the writer wants to say.

> Dear Ms. Carelli:
>
> This is in reference to your recent email which has been received and forwarded to the appropriate department.
>
> Please be advised that your complaint will be prioritized immediately and you will be contacted when the nature of the difficulty has been ascertained. Action will then be taken in accordance with the facts.
>
> We regret this unfortunate occurrence. Please do not hesitate to contact this writer if further assistance is required.
>
> Sincerely,
>
> Joyce Ellensby

It's hard to follow, isn't it? Here's what the writer may have meant.

> Dear Ms. Carelli:
>
> Thank you for your email. I am sorry we have misplaced your loan documents, delaying your loan approval.
>
> James Nguyen manages our Research Department; searching for your documents is a high priority for his team. He will send me a report within three days.
>
> I will call you by next Friday with an update on your application's status.
>
> Sincerely,
>
> Joyce Ellensby

The revised email is more concise, even though it includes some new information. The new email also gets the message across more clearly because the writer uses active, specific language, and she uses plain English instead of business jargon.

Use active language

Passive language can weaken your writing, confuse your readers, and make your sentences longer. In contrast, active language focuses your readers' attention and increases the impact of your message.

As you can see in the following examples of active language, the actor comes before the action. To use active language, say *who* acts, and not just what the action is. We've underlined the actor in the following revisions and set the action in bold.

PASSIVE: The project **was managed** by <u>John</u>.

ACTIVE: <u>John</u> **managed** the project.

                      (unnecessary words: "was" and "by") (actor: John)
                      (action: managed)

PASSIVE: The design document **has been completed** by <u>the team.</u>

ACTIVE: <u>The team</u> **has completed** the design document.

PASSIVE: A safety plan **was prepared** and **distributed** to employees by <u>the committee</u>.

ACTIVE: <u>The committee</u> **prepared** a safety plan and **distributed** it to employees.

Sometimes the actor in a sentence is implied rather than spelled out. For instance, in the sentence "Prepare a safety plan," the implied subject is "<u>you.</u>" (I.e., "I'm asking or telling you to prepare a safety plan.")

When you give instructions, it's particularly important to say clearly what you want your readers to do. It can be frustrating and confusing to try to follow instructions in passive language.

PASSIVE: The water **should be measured** every 35 minutes.

ACTIVE: <u>The technician</u> **should measure** the water every 35 minutes.

— OR —

Measure the water every 35 minutes.

(an implied "<u>you</u>")

These revisions make the passive language active by implying or stating an actor. Either the technician or the reader should measure the water.

Here's another example.

PASSIVE: The cover of the printer **should be lifted,** the ink cartridges that **have been emptied should be removed,** and the new ink cartridges should be **opened, prepared,** and **inserted** in the appropriate slots.

ACTIVE: [implied "<u>you</u>"] **Lift** the printer cover, **remove** the empty cartridges, **open** and **prepare** the new cartridges, and **insert** them into the appropriate slot.

In this revision, the implied actor — an implied "<u>you</u>," or the reader — now appears before the action of lifting the cover and removing the cartridges.

The next two examples also show how to revise a passive-language sentence by adding a missing subject or actor.

PASSIVE: The door **was found** unlocked three times during the past month.

ACTIVE: The security guard **found** the door unlocked three times during the past month.

•

PASSIVE: It **would be appreciated** if the report **could be delivered** to me on Monday.

ACTIVE: I **would appreciate** it if you **would deliver** the report to me on Monday.

The actor in a sentence isn't always a person. Both these sentences feature active language:

ACTIVE: The plan **is** flawed.

ACTIVE: The weather **prevented** us from going out.

PRACTICE 4.1

Below or on some note paper, revise these sentences so they become active, direct, and clear. The first step is to identify an actor; feel free to invent one. Also feel free to rearrange sentence elements.

1.   The research project is being conducted by the News Department.

2.   A copy of the approval must be stapled to the request before it is forwarded to the Accounting Office.

3.   The new design is attached for your review and its return by March 15 would be appreciated.

4.   An investigation will be conducted by Andrea Russo into the concern voiced by Mr. Szabo.

5.   Reservations for the conference can be made by telephoning Tom Woo at Extension 4732 before December 1.

ANSWERS

Your revisions should look something like the sentences below. The original version appears first, followed by the revision. Make sure that the actor comes before the action in your revisions.

1. **The research project is being conducted by the News Department.**

   The News Department is conducting the research project.

2. **A copy of the approval must be stapled to the request before it is forwarded to the Accounting Office.**

   You must staple a copy of the approval to the request before you forward it to the Accounting Office.

3. **The new design is attached for your review and its return by March 15 would be appreciated.**

   [an implied you] Please review the design and return it by March 15.

4. **An investigation will be conducted by Andrea Russo into the concern voiced by Mr. Szabo.**

   Mr. Szabo voiced a concern, and Andrea Russo will investigate it.

5. **Reservations for the conference can be made by telephoning Tom Woo at Extension 4732 before December 1.**

   You can make reservations for the conference by telephoning Tom Woo at Extension 4732 before December 1.

   —OR—

   [implied you] Call Tom Woo at Extension 4732 before December 1 to make reservations for the conference.

PRACTICE 4.2

Do you use too much passive language when you write? Look through some sample documents you've written for passive, indirect sentences. If you find any, write two of them below. Then revise the sentences to be active and direct. If you don't find any passive sentences, go on to the next section of this lesson.

If you're not sure whether a sentence is passive or active, try underlining the actor and circling the action on a printout. The language is passive if you can't find an actor (including an implied "you") or if the actor comes after the action.

ORIGINAL

_____

_____

_____

_____

REVISION

_____

_____

_____

_____

ORIGINAL

_____

_____

_____

_____

REVISION

_____

_____

_____

Use specific language

Specific language makes your writing easier to read, while vague language paints an unclear picture. The more specific your language is, the less guesswork and effort your readers will need to understand your message.

VAGUE:	Some time ago, the building was destroyed in a disaster.
SPECIFIC:	In 1994, fire destroyed the apartment house.

VAGUE:	Our group went to Los Angeles for a meeting.
SPECIFIC:	Our project team flew to Los Angeles to meet with Harriet Allen, the system designer.

VAGUE:	Ask the client to complete the paperwork in a timely manner.
SPECIFIC:	Ask the client to complete the new account application form within ten working days.

It can show consideration when you supply your readers with precise information. Vague language can require them to guess at the meanings behind your word choices, so try to use words and phrases like the ones listed here to make your writing less vague and more specific.

VAGUE:	SPECIFIC:
vehicle	car
car	convertible
equipment	computer
computer	laptop, tablet
went	walked; ran; drove
traveled	flew; took the train; sailed
contacted	called; spoke to; visited
some	five
recently	yesterday
in a timely manner	by August 15; within two weeks

PRACTICE 4.3

Underline the vague, general words and phrases in these sentences. Then use your imagination to fill in details and revise the sentences so they communicate specific, useful information.

1. Recently, we looked at a structure that may be suitable for our needs.

   _____

   _____

   _____

2. During the incident, Ms. Brown sustained multiple injuries to her upper torso and limbs.

   _____

   _____

   _____

3. We have identified a few items to be discussed at the meeting, so please leave considerable time in your schedule.

   _____

   _____

   _____

   _____

ANSWERS

Your revisions should look something like these; the original version appears first, followed by the revision. Your revisions may have very different new details. The original words are vague and imprecise, while more concrete terms replace them here.

1. **Recently, we looked at a structure that may be suitable for our needs.**

   Last week we looked at a four-story building that may be big enough for our new machine polishers.

2. **During the incident, Ms. Brown sustained multiple injuries to her upper torso and limbs.**

   During the fall, Ms. Brown's chest, shoulders, and arms were scratched and cut.

3. **We have identified a few items to be discussed at the meeting, so please leave considerable time in your schedule.**

   At the meeting, we will discuss the next conference, the move to the new building, and the new staff position. Please leave at least three hours in your schedule.

PRACTICE 4.4

Check your own writing for vague words and phrases. If you find any, write two of the phrases in the space below and revise them to be more specific and clear.

ORIGINAL

_____

_____

_____

REVISION

_____

_____

_____

ORIGINAL

_____

_____

_____

REVISION

_____

_____

_____

Use plain English

Do you ever have to read something very slowly because the writer used unnecessarily formal or uncommon words when everyday language would have gotten the point across?

Pompous language can confuse, intimidate, amuse, or annoy your readers. Plain English communicates your message more reliably. Stuffy words and phrases can force readers to mentally translate your writing into everyday language, which can waste valuable time and cause misunderstandings.

How long does it take for you to read this paragraph and understand it?

> Per your request, enclosed herewith are documents concerning the above-mentioned project. Please review said documents and return them to this office prior to January 15. We will then initiate the process of implementing the requested system modifications.

See how much easier the paragraph is to read when it's written in plain English?

> As you asked, I am sending a description of the Acme project. Please read the description and send it back to me before January 15. We will then begin the system modifications.

Pompous language gets in the way of your message, so look for ordinary words that communicate your message as simply and directly as possible.

PRACTICE 4.5

Sometimes, the words in this list are the best, most precise words to use. But writers often use these words when simpler language would communicate more clearly. What ordinary words or phrases would be good alternatives to the words listed here? Use a thesaurus or dictionary if you're not sure.

1. prior to

2. subsequent to

3. utilize

4. modifications

5. enhance

6. beneficial

7. supplemental

8. magnitude

9. supersede

10. augment

11. heretofore

12. parameters

13. commence

14. endeavor

15. forthwith

ANSWERS

Here are some simpler word choices. You may have different, equally correct answers.

1.	**prior to**	before
2.	**subsequent to**	after; following
3.	**utilize**	use
4.	**modifications**	changes
5.	**enhance**	improve
6.	**beneficial**	helpful
7.	**supplemental**	extra
8.	**magnitude**	size
9.	**supersede**	replace
10.	**augment**	increase; add to
11.	**heretofore**	before; until now
12.	**parameters**	boundaries; limits
13.	**commence**	begin; start
14.	**endeavor**	try
15.	**forthwith**	immediately

PRACTICE 4.6

Use plain English and active language to revise these sentences.

1.   Division managers are hereupon requested to facilitate the implementation of the aforementioned program by forwarding details of their personnel requirements.

_____

_____

_____

_____

2.   The injuries sustained by the passengers during the accident were the result of their failure to use the vehicle's restraining elements.

_____

_____

_____

_____

3.   Enclosed herewith is a heretofore-unseen listing of procedures that must be implemented by our team immediately.

_____

_____

_____

_____

ANSWERS

Your revisions may look like these.

1. **Division managers are hereupon requested to facilitate the implementation of the aforementioned program by forwarding details of their personnel requirements.**

    Please help us get this program started by letting us know how many people you need to complete the job.

    $-$ OR $-$

    To help us get this program off the ground, please send us a list of your division's personnel needs.

2. **The injuries sustained by the passengers during the accident were the result of their failure to use the vehicle's restraining elements.**

    The passengers were injured in the accident because they didn't use seat belts.

3. **Enclosed herewith is a heretofore-unseen listing of procedures that must be implemented by our team immediately.**

    Here is a list of new procedures that our team must implement immediately.

    $-$ OR $-$

    Please begin using these procedures at once.

PRACTICE 4.7

Look for examples of language in your own writing that would be more effective as plain English. Underline any words or phrases you find, write two of them below, and revise them.

ORIGINAL

_____

_____

_____

_____

REVISION

_____

_____

_____

_____

ORIGINAL

_____

_____

_____

_____

REVISION

_____

_____

_____

_____

Avoid jargon

Business writing is full of jargon — words, phrases, abbreviations, and acronyms that make sense only to people who are used to business language, or who share a particular job.

Sometimes professionals give new meanings to familiar words, and sometimes they invent new jargon terms. Some of these terms enter mainstream language: bankers' automated teller machines from the 1970s are today's ATMs. *Networking* is another business term that has become widespread and very useful.

However, jargon damages business writing when it's difficult for readers to understand. You should define any terms that may be new to your readers. Here are a few examples of business jargon that many readers would find confusing:

buy-in: agreement on what to do

drill down: examine more closely

drink the Kool-Aid: accept without thinking

ducks in a row: elements of a careful plan

leverage (as a verb): take full advantage of an asset or situation

(For more examples, see Max Mallet, Brett Nelson, and Chris Steiner's "The Most Annoying, Pretentious and Useless Business Jargon," *Forbes* online, January 26, 2012.)

Here are three kinds of jargon you should usually avoid when you're not writing to a coworker:

Everyday words used in a nonstandard way:

We plan a campaign to <u>migrate</u> customers to our bank.

Words your reader won't find in a current dictionary:

We hope to <u>maximalize</u> our marketing potential.

Potentially unclear acronyms:

Next year's goals include increasing the <u>BOCSF</u>, establishing a <u>RADIT</u>, and improving the <u>FAJ</u>.

SPELL OUT ACRONYMS

It's fine to use an acronym your readers may not know if you spell out the words the first time you use the term, followed by the acronym in parentheses. Afterward, just use the acronym. For instance, the following sentences could be part of an email to a new intern in an office:

I'd like you to read the attached request for proposal (RFP)....

Let's discuss the RFP on Monday; after that, I'd like you to start writing a response to it.

PRACTICE 4.8

Look for examples of jargon in your own writing. If you find any, underline the words and then write them below. Translate two of the jargon words into plain English.

JARGON

_____

TRANSLATION

_____

JARGON

_____

TRANSLATION

_____

APPLY WHAT YOU'VE LEARNED

To apply what you learned in this lesson, revise the following paragraphs so the language is active, specific, and in plain English. Feel free to invent details.

> Enclosed herewith is the information requested by you in your recent communication with the undersigned subsequent to your recent purchase of our computer system. It is our belief that the enhancements described therein would be beneficial to the efficiency of your organization by making it possible to increase the amount of data processed within a given time period.
>
> It is our policy to endeavor to provide the optimum service possible to our customers. Please be advised that should you have additional questions or concerns, every attempt will be made to provide a response in a timely manner.

_____

_____

_____

_____

_____

_____

_____

_____

_____

_____

_____

_____

ANSWERS

Here's one way to revise the paragraphs. The details of your revision will probably differ.

> As you asked, I am sending a description of the improvements we plan to make to the Model 603A computer system you purchased from us last year. We believe these improvements will help your organization process at least 15 percent more data each month.
>
> We try to provide the best possible service to our customers. Please let me know if you have any more questions or concerns, and I will do my best to address them within five working days.

Apply 10 proofreading tips

Save time for proofreading as the final activity after you've edited and revised your writing for the larger issues of organization, content, and tone. The following 10 proofreading tips work well with any professional document.

1. You proofread most effectively when you have distance from a document. So take breaks between writing the first draft, revising it, and proofreading it.

2. Try reading your work out loud, and ask yourself if the sentences sound correct when you hear them.

3. Some writers proofread backward — from the end of the document to the beginning. Disrupting the narrative flow can help you see the individual sentences and paragraphs in new ways.

4. Run your spell-checker carefully and slowly, correcting misspellings one by one. Be especially careful to check spellings for distinctive names for products, organizations, and individuals.

5. Try separate proofreading scans for separate grammar and punctuation challenges. For example, if you know you find apostrophes especially challenging, then read through your document one time looking just for apostrophe errors. If you know you tend to confuse the words *comprise* and *compose* in your technical reports, then check the dictionary and type those words into the word processor's Find function. Then you won't have to hunt for them separately.

6. Proofread several times, taking breaks to gain some helpful distance from the document. Proofread once, call a friend or get some coffee, and then proofread again.

7. Zoom in so that the text is very large — making errors easier to see. Or try proofreading from a printed page after you've written on a screen. The differences can help you see your document with fresh eyes.

8. If any document is important to your career, then ask your manager or a coworker to proofread it after you've given it your best shot. Other people may catch further nonstandard English, or they may simply help you see your document in a new light. Others' feedback often helps us communicate more effectively through our writing.

9. In a letter, make sure you haven't misspelled any information in the date or address blocks. Don't overlook these words just because they seem familiar.

10. And don't forget to proof headings! It's especially easy to overlook headings because they're signposts that point you toward the information that follows them.

LESSON 4 REVIEW

Fill in the blanks with the correct word or phrase. The page numbers for each topic are listed in parentheses.

1. In active language, the _____ comes before the _____ (page 119).

2. _____ makes your writing easier to read, while vague language paints an unclear picture (125).

3. Pompous language can confuse, intimidate, amuse, or annoy your readers. _____ _____ communicates your message more reliably (129).

4. Business writing is full of _____ — that is, words, phrases, abbreviations, and acronyms that make sense only to people who are used to business language, or who share a particular job (135).

5   WRITE EFFECTIVE EMAIL

INTRODUCTION

Now you're ready to apply the planning and writing skills you've reviewed in the last four lessons to one type of professional writing: email.

Advances in electronic communications since the 1990s have radically changed the way businesspeople work. Yet age-old writing challenges can prevent email from being as clear, concise, and effective as it should be.

Businesspeople still send email that's confusing or offensive, or that lands them and their organizations in court. Like any other kind of business writing, professional email requires thought and attention.

OBJECTIVES

This lesson will help you master the following challenges:

- Write clear, concise email that quickly conveys the information readers need and gets the results you want
- Use email to convey a professional image of yourself and your organization
- Avoid trouble by recognizing what topics and information are and are not appropriate

WHAT YOU'LL NEED:

- The writing plan that you completed over the course of Lesson 1 (pages 56–57)
- Ten sample emails you've written for your job

Email is ideal for quick messages to transmit information, ask and respond to questions, and make requests. Email may not seem to call for the same kind of planning that a hard-copy memo, letter, or report would. But email is still business writing.

Even if you have only a simple message to convey, you'll get better results if you stop and think about why you're writing, identify what information you want to pass along, and decide what you want the recipient to do.

Is email the appropriate choice for this message?

What if you received the two emails below? Is email the best way — or the right way — to communicate the information? Why or why not?

> Dear Larissa,
>
> This is to notify you that you have come in more than half an hour late four days out of the past seven. We spoke about this issue during your last performance evaluation.
>
> Sincerely,
>
> Daniel

.

> Billy,
>
> I know how you feel about that invoice. I almost screamed at the finances woman when she kept telling me she didn't have it. I can't find my copy either, and I know you sent me at least two of them.
>
> Could you please send me copies ONE MORE TIME? This will get solved today, or I start building a death-ray laser gun out of office supplies. Sorry for the tirade!
>
> By the way, I heard that your manager is thinking about leaving the company. His daughter told my daughter in gymnastics class.
>
> Better keep it to yourself, but I thought you'd like to know.
>
> Parker

You probably agree that email wasn't the appropriate choice for either of those messages. Daniel's message to Larissa addresses performance problems, which should always remain confidential and are best addressed in person. And Parker used email to vent her feelings, something she might regret later. She also passed on a rumor and dangerously assumed that Billy would keep it confidential.

The question "Is it convenient?" should never trump the question "Should I send this in the first place?" Email is too public for some messages: it's more like sending a postcard than sealing a letter in an envelope.

Remember that email is just one communication medium, and that a phone call, meeting, or printed memo or letter may be a better way to deliver your message.

Consider the consequences

Here are three kinds of messages that are often too risky to go into an email:

- **NEGATIVE FEELINGS.** Face-to-face interaction is vital when your message might upset another person. Sometimes it's too easy to throw negative feelings into an email and send it off without pausing to think how the recipient might react.

- **JOKES ABOUT OTHERS.** The casualness of email also makes it easy to forget that email can be the wrong place to poke fun at an individual or a group. Something that seems funny to you could offend others who see the message. Offensive emails can get you and your organization into trouble.

- **COMPLEX INFORMATION.** An email is not the best way to convey complex information, which is hard to read on a screen and may look different in a printout. Try to send complex information as an attached file, instead of in the body of your message, and use your email to describe or summarize the file's contents.

THINK ABOUT IT ...

Have you ever received an inappropriate email at your organization? How did you feel about it? Did other people see it? Were there any consequences? Did it affect a professional relationship?

In the last month, have you sent emails with messages more appropriate to a different communication method — or that you shouldn't have sent at all?

Apply Lesson 1's five steps to email

Think about how you read email. Do you sit back with a cup of coffee and ponder every word?

Most business readers are likely to read only the first few lines before deciding whether an email merits any more of their time. If it does, they scan the rest of the message to pick out the important points.

This habit of fast reading makes it vital to plan your messages. The five steps you learned in Lesson 1 work as well for email as for any other kind of document:

1. Think about what you're going to write from the reader's point of view.

2. Decide what you want to accomplish: is your primary purpose to persuade readers, or to inform them?

3. Compose a key sentence that expresses your most important message.

4. List the facts and ideas that will accomplish your purpose.

5. Group your ideas into categories.

Remember that communication is a two-way process: your email recipients must receive your message and be able to understand it. So never neglect **STEP 1** for an email. Stop to think about your recipients' point of view as carefully as you would if you sat down to write a letter.

- Sometimes you'll need to send the same email to several people or a large group. Ask yourself whether those readers' needs, interests, and concerns are similar enough for one message to be appropriate for all of them.

- If not, you'll get better results by writing more than one email and tailoring your messages to different audiences:

  - You might write one longer email to give a few readers background context for a topic.

  - And you might write another shorter email to readers who already have that contextual information.

When you don't know your email recipients, weigh factors such as the type of organization they work for, their positions, and their relationships with you and your organization. Consider **STEPS 2 THROUGH 4** for each email you send:

- **STEP 2.** Like any other business document, email is far more clear when you determine your purpose before you start writing. If your reader can't grasp your purpose, your message is much less likely to get results.

- **STEP 3.** Decide on your single, main point and send a quick, clear signal to readers who may only have time to skim your email. Frame that point as a key sentence, and put it at the beginning. Then expand on your main point with specific ideas, using the journalistic triangle from page 78 to go from a big picture to smaller details.

- **STEP 4.** As you plan your email, list the ideas that either deliver information you want readers to have or explain why they should do what you'd like them to do. Also stop and think about exactly what information readers need:

  - For email to be useful, you should answer all the readers' questions

  - And for email to be concise, you should answer *only* those questions

- **STEP 5.** Since emails should be easy to read, it's especially important to group your ideas into logical categories that make sense at first glance. With some planning, you'll offer your readers well-organized messages with just enough information to accomplish your purpose, every time you click Send.

STRIKE THE RIGHT TONE

Email is informal, and we tend to use a casual style for it. Sometimes our writing style for email is the same at work as it is with our friends. But it can be a serious mistake to be too casual. Here are six tones that are always appropriate to strike in any work email.

BE POLITE. When you write email at work, adopt a polite tone and err on the side of writing like a formal letter. Starting your email with a formal opening such as "Dear Ms. Brown," or "Hello Ellen" can help you maintain a polite tone. Your readers may reciprocate the respect you offer them in the form of respect for you and your organization.

BE CONSIDERATE. Write "please" when you ask for something (which is always a form of writing to persuade), and write "thank you" when someone completes a task.

MAKE OPEN REQUESTS WHEN YOU NEED TO. When you need something, ask a question and be explicit about what you need. Your reader may not understand you if you bury a request in a long email or don't clearly explain yourself.

GIVE PEOPLE TIME TO REPLY. Give people ample time to reply before you send a follow-up message. Ask them when they might be able to reply. Make it clear that you know they have other duties by writing statements such as, "I know that you're busy trying to finish this quarter. Could you please let me know by Wednesday?"

"URGENT" SHOULD MEAN TRULY URGENT. If it's really urgent, then say so — as the first word of your subject line. However, your readers will start ignoring you if you flag half your emails with double exclamation points.

BE POSITIVE. Keep your language and the tone of your writing positive. Negative language or sarcastic writing usually don't work in email: they're too easy to misunderstand.

PRACTICE 5.1

The tone in these email sentences is problematic. Look for more engaging ways to rephrase these ideas, writing your answers below or on some note paper.

1. Let me know if you do not understand.

2. I know that you are busy, but send it to me as soon as you can.

3. Call me with your comments, which may include information that I need.

4. I look forward to completing this matter.

ANSWERS

Your revisions may vary from these.

1. **Let me know if you do not understand.**

   Please let me know if I can further explain any of this information.

2. **I know that you are busy, but send it to me as soon as you can.**

   I know that you are busy, but I would appreciate it if you would send it to me as soon as you can.

3. **Call me with your comments, which may include information that I need.**

   Please call me with your comments: I may benefit from hearing the information you can give me.

4. **I look forward to completing this matter.**

   I look forward to completing this project with your help.

Launch your message

Email can save a lot of time, but it raises concerns that don't come up in other business documents:

- How do I handle the CC line?

- What should be on the subject line?

- Do I always have to use a salutation? A closing? Complete sentences?

- How do I format my message so it's easy to read?

- Do my punctuation and grammar have to be perfect?

These questions don't have quick and easy answers. But the tips and techniques in the following sections will help you send email that achieves your goals and satisfies your readers' needs.

Reread your email for sense

Keep yourself in the recipient's shoes, and reread your whole email before you send it. Make any necessary changes to the content of the message right away — before you fuss with the formatting, subject line, or other components. If you find any unnecessary information, then delete it. If you forgot anything essential, then add it.

Stop yourself if you start to rewrite the message, move things around, or add a lot of new information. Remember that you've already mapped out your purpose, audience, main point, key sentence, and the questions the email needs to answer.

When you reread for sense, also check the tone. Is the email too abrupt? Too casual? Too formal? Not friendly enough?

ABRUPT:	Get me the revisions by Thursday.
POLITE:	Please be sure to send me the revisions by Thursday.
CORDIAL:	I would appreciate your making sure I get the revisions by Thursday.
CASUAL:	Got a lot on my plate right now — not sure I can take on a new gig.
PROFESSIONAL:	I'm very busy at the moment, and I'm not sure I can take on a new project.
STUFFY:	Prior to July 23, payments can be sent only through the Postal Service. Subsequent to that date, payments must be made through our website.
STRAIGHTFORWARD:	Before July 23, you can make payments only by mail. You can make payments on our website after July 23.

Don't use all-capital or all-lowercase letters in your email paragraphs. They're hard to read and, respectively, they sound either too demanding or too casual.

Make the email easy to read

How easily can you follow this email?

> Hi, Laura,
>
> The total contribution you've made for this tax year is $7,200. The maximum contribution for the year is $11,000 plus an additional $1,000 if you are age 50 or older. If Craig wishes to contribute the maximum, he can contribute $4,800 for the rest of the year (12,000 – 7,200 = 4,800). If he can get the Salary Reduction Agreement form to me by Tuesday, we can take advantage of the last three months in this tax year (4,800 divided by 3 = $1,600). Next year's maximum is $12,000 plus an additional $2,000 for people age 50 or older. Our tax year begins with the December pay period (the check that's issued on January 1). I hope this information is helpful.
>
> Best wishes,
>
> Pierre

It doesn't look like Pierre thought about about how his message would look on a computer screen — or on a handheld device. Even though the message is well written, it takes effort to understand it.

Notice how much easier the message is to read when it's broken down into short paragraphs, with a blank line between each one:

> Hi, Laura,
>
> The total contribution you've made for this tax year is $7,200. The maximum contribution for the year is $11,000, plus an additional $1,000 if you are age 50 or older.
>
> If Craig wishes to contribute the maximum, he can contribute $4,800 for the rest of the year ($12,000 − $7,200 = $4,800). If he can get the Salary Reduction Agreement form to me by Tuesday, we can take advantage of the last three months in this tax year ($4,800 divided by 3 = $1,600).
>
> Next year's maximum is $12,000 plus an additional $2,000 for people age 50 or older. Our tax year begins with the December pay period (the check that's issued on January 1).
>
> I hope this information is helpful.
>
> Best wishes,
>
> Pierre

When a message is clearly written and presented, the reader should be able to grasp the important information by quickly scanning it. Keep these points in mind for all email:

- Short sentences and paragraphs are easier to read than long ones
- Lists are easier to read than sentences and paragraphs
- Information is easier to follow when there's space between list items and paragraphs

THREE QUICK TIPS

Here are three rules of thumb for email:

- Send only one thought per email
- Don't use email for bad news
- Try not to use email to say no

CAN AN EMAIL PARAGRAPH BE ONLY ONE SENTENCE LONG?

Sure it can. One-sentence paragraphs are fine in emails as long as each sentence communicates a complete thought.

Mark,

As you asked, I'll make the necessary changes to the project timetable and send you a revised calendar by next Friday.

Deanna

•

Marketing Team,

We've scheduled the telephone meeting for 10:30 a.m. tomorrow, May 3.

Billy

Consider your salutation

Email doesn't need to follow all the same rules as formal business correspondence. But a salutation or greeting is like saying "Hi" or "Hello" when you begin a conversation. It helps you do three things:

- Establish a personal contact
- Show readers that the email is meant for them when you use the reader's name
- Set a positive tone

Salutations or greetings can be more formal or more informal, depending on the situation. Talk with your manager or colleagues or use your best judgment so you'll sound relaxed enough yet respectful enough.

Should I include a salutation?

You should usually include a salutation. You can leave it off in a back-and-forth email exchange, and sometimes when you provide a brief answer to a question. But an email can seem abrupt if the writer emails you out of the blue without any greeting to plunge straight into dates, actions, and dollar amounts.

Your company may have a policy to determine which kinds of salutation you use. Otherwise, you can use the ones that follow:

Dear Mr. Wolinsky,	Hi, Bob,	Dear Bob,	Hello, Bob,
Bob,	Dear clients,	To my clients:	Hi, team,
Hi, everyone,	Hello, associates		

Should I use commas in salutations?

People often omit the comma between the "Hi" or "Hello" and the person's name for informal salutations:

Hi, Bob,

Hi Bob,

Either form is fine. Be sure, however, to type the comma after the person's name.

You usually need a formal salutation ("Dear _____") only for people outside your organization. But there are exceptions. If you're writing to someone senior to you, such as a director or chairman of the board, it might be more appropriate to write "Dear Ms. Moreno" or "Dear Director" instead of "Hi, Allison."

Are you writing to a colleague or friend for the first time that day or week? Use an informal salutation or greeting, or just begin with the person's name. It's usually better to use a more formal salutation when you write to someone you've never met, never spoken with on the phone, or never communicated with by email.

When you reply to an email, note the way the person has addressed you. If he or she chose a formal salutation, you should probably use a formal salutation in return. People outside the US tend to be more formal in business settings. When you write to someone in another country, you might want to use a formal salutation for at least your first message.

COLONS IN SALUTATIONS?

Another common question is whether to use a colon after a formal salutation, the way you would if you were writing a business letter.

Dear Mr. O'Connor:

The evolving style is to use a comma instead of a colon.

Dear Mr. O'Connor,

Unless your organization's style guide or your manager address this topic, do what feels right to you.

PRACTICE 5.2

Do you ever receive email that has no salutation or greeting? Under what circumstances does that seem okay?

What kind of salutation or greeting do you normally use in the emails you send? How do you decide what to type? Write your answers in the space below.

_____

_____

_____

_____

_____

_____

_____

_____

_____

_____

_____

PRACTICE 5.3

1. Check the salutations on ten recent email messages you've sent and received. Are they appropriate for the situation? Too formal? Too casual? Too abrupt? How would you change them? Write three of the original salutations or greetings on the lines below along with any changes you'd make.

    ORIGINALS   **REVISIONS**

    _____

    _____

    _____

    _____

    _____

    _____

    _____

    _____

    _____

2. Look at five recent emails you've sent and five you've received. Do they have useful closings and signatures? What changes might have helped?

3. Do you already have a signature file that automatically adds a signature block to your email? Do you have at least one alternate signature? If so, review those files to see whether they need any changes.

The exercise continues on the next page.

PRACTICE 5.3, continued

4. Look through a magazine or some news articles, and jot down some headlines that draw your attention. Notice whether the headline writer gave you a quick preview of the article content in those few words, and write out the best three headlines below.

   _____

   _____

   _____

5. Look at the subject lines from five emails you've sent and five you've received. Do they meet this chapter's criteria for a well-written subject line? If not, how could you revise them so they'd be more effective? Write three of the original subject lines and their revisions below.

ORIGINAL

   _____

REVISION

   _____

ORIGINAL

   _____

REVISION

   _____

ORIGINAL

   _____

REVISION

   _____

The exercise concludes on the next page.

PRACTICE 5.3 (continued)

6. Write out effective subject lines based on these three scenarios:

   Simon needs someone to volunteer to provide administrative assistance for the Heart Association project.

   SUBJECT LINE: _____

   Melissa can't attend the Verizon meeting on February 6, but she wants someone to attend in her place and take notes.

   SUBJECT LINE: _____

   Grisha believes that the draft of the Clorox presentation needs a lot more work.

   SUBJECT LINE: _____

7. Do you regularly send email to groups? Review the distribution list for at least one of those groups. Add or remove addresses to make sure that the right people — and only the right people — get those messages.

SEND DIFFERENT SIGNALS WITH CC AND REPLY ALL

Think carefully about whether you should click Reply All to send a single message to all the people who've received an email along with you. Reply All works best when every single recipient might need to respond to your message.

CCing can send a valuable signal: that you don't believe a CCed person is likely to need to reply to your new email. A person who's CCed on an email may feel glad to be informed, but also glad not to have any duty to respond.

Put a group of readers on the To line only when all of them are likely to be responsible for writing you back. CC one or more people when they may be interested in a message, but aren't likely to need to take action.

In that case, reserve the To line for your primary reader, who should take action or should write back to acknowledge your information. In this scenario, the CCed people are still in the loop, but they can remain spectators and move on to other business.

Consider your closing

A closing is like the period that ends a sentence: it lets the reader know you're done. Closings can be polite and efficient by letting readers know they've reached the end of the message. Like the salutation, the closing can be formal, informal, or casual.

FORMAL: Sincerely, Regards, Yours truly,

LESS FORMAL: Best wishes, Best, Warm regards, Regards, Thank you,

CASUAL: Thanks, See you soon, Enjoy your weekend,

Choose a salutation and a closing that complement each other. For brief messages to friends and colleagues, it's usually fine to close with only your name, initials, or signature block. But keep in mind that this kind of closing can have an abrupt tone, as in these two examples:

Joseph,

UPS picked up the package today. It should arrive by next Tuesday.

Sheila

•

Thanks for the update, Brendon — will let you know if I need more details.

J.

MATCH YOUR CLOSING TO YOUR BUSINESS GOALS

Remember that business writing always has a purpose. The planning process helps you decide exactly what information you need your reader to grasp or what action you'd like her or him to take. Your closing paragraph represents one last opportunity to stamp an email or other document with your purpose.

TRY IT: Look through some documents you've written for your job — especially documents that didn't get results for you. Did your closing sentences or closing paragraph help you and your reader accomplish necessary business goals? Or could a more focused conclusion have helped you and the reader conduct your business more effectively?

Consider your signature

An email without a signature is like a voicemail message without a name or phone number: the unspoken assumption is that the other person knows who you are and how to reach you. But someone you call may not recognize your voice, have your number handy, or have a call-back button. In a similar way, your email recipient might not recognize your email address or know your number.

To avoid these problems, consider automatically including your name and number in all emails. Repeating your email address in a signature block can make it easier for people to find you if they're not replying immediately. If you use more than one email address, make sure the address on the From line is the one you want people to use.

Worried about whether your message was received?

Sometime you need to know that someone received your email, but you don't need a fuller reply. In those cases, add a line requesting a reply at the beginning or end of the email, such as "Please let me know when you get this message."

Announce your attachments

Here are four rules of thumb for attachments:

- **ASK WHETHER ALL READERS NEED THE ATTACHMENT.** Sometimes only your primary reader needs an attachment — the person named on the To line and not the people on the CC line. In those cases, you might want to send the others a separate email without the attachment — especially if it's large.

- **ALWAYS TELL YOUR READERS WHEN YOU ATTACH A FILE TO YOUR EMAIL.** Otherwise, they might delete, forward, or save the message before noticing an important addition that they need.

- **SAVE YOUR READERS TIME BY TELLING THEM WHAT THE ATTACHMENT IS, AND CLEARLY EXPLAIN WHAT YOU EXPECT THEM TO DO WITH IT.** Don't force them to open it or wait till they get back to a computer just to find out what you've sent them. If the attachment is long and complex, consider summarizing it briefly in the body of the email.

- **CONSIDER SENDING A LINK INSTEAD OF A FILE.** It takes time to open and read an attachment, and some devices don't have the programs or applications readers would need to open a file. You can save readers time and help them use email when they're away from their computers by uploading files to an online storage service and sending a download link instead of the file itself.

Consider your subject line

Remember that each subject line you send may have to compete for attention with dozens or hundreds of other subject lines in an inbox that's bursting at the seams. An effective subject line can dramatically increase your odds of being heard.

Imagine a news website with no headlines and just first paragraphs of text arranged in rows. How would you know what stories you wanted to read? A well-written email subject line is like the headline for a news article:

- It draws the reader's attention

- It tells the reader what the subject is

- It gives the reader a reason to open the text

Here are seven guidelines to keep your subject lines effective.

1. **MAKE YOUR SUBJECT LINE COMPELLING.** A subject line is also your first and most important opportunity to get your message across. The best subject lines summarize and introduce email contents while also piquing readers' interest. Notice the difference between the original and revised subject lines in the following examples:

ORIGINAL:	Changes
REVISION:	Health benefits will change on Dec. 1: Please enroll
ORIGINAL:	Planning date?
REVISION:	Planning project: Is meeting on Apr. 2, 6 or 9?
VAGUE:	Report
SPECIFIC:	Robotix computer upgrade project report
NOT DESCRIPTIVE:	Budget
DESCRIPTIVE:	Marketing budget increased 10%

    These revised subject lines hook the readers' attention with specific information, questions, or requests. The lines tell readers what each email is about, and they'll also enable readers to find each message again later by searching for a key word or phrase.

2. **AVOID CERTAIN WORDS.** Some words or phrases can route your message to a spam folder, where your reader will probably never see it. Here are a few examples:

> For your eyes only   Confirmation of order
>
> Look at this!

3. **AVOID EXCLAMATION POINTS.** Rely on good word choices instead of punctuation to hook readers' attention. In a misguided attempt to call attention to their emails, some writers use extravagant punctuation to try to make their subject lines more punchy:

> Only 3 days left to apply!
>
> Your response required!!!

Exclamation points can send your message to the spam folder. If an email really is urgent, your system might let you flag it or mark it in some way. Better yet, make a phone call to let the recipient know it's coming and needs immediate attention.

It's unfair to mislead readers by conveying a false sense of urgency. It can also undermine your credibility to use exclamation points for humor in work emails.

4. **NEVER LEAVE THE SUBJECT LINE BLANK.** A blank line is useless to the recipient and may look like spam.

5. **MAKE SUBJECT LINES CONCISE AND CLEAR.** A compelling subject line gets the message across without unnecessary words or obscure abbreviations.

> **WORDY AND CONFUSING:**
>
> This msg inclds new details abt our shoes + accessories
>
> **CONCISE AND CLEAR:**
>
> Introducing free returns on shoes and accessories

6. **CONSIDER THE LENGTH.** Long subject lines are often truncated, especially on handheld devices. If you can't avoid a long subject line, make sure the key information appears in the first few words.

7. **CHANGE YOUR EMAILS' SUBJECT LINES WHEN THE SUBJECT CHANGES IN A REPLY TO AN EARLIER EMAIL.** For instance, a series of emails could change subjects in this way:

   - Starting out as a *full* list of project activities

   - Then turning into a debate over the best completion date for *one* activity

   - And then turning into a discussion of *an unrelated event* that makes one completion date unrealistic

In a back-and-forth multireply conversation, simply pay special attention to the evolving subjects. If the subject remains the same, you won't need to change the subject line.

But it's confusing when an original subject line no longer reflects the topic of the latest email — for instance, by still reading "Project activities" when the topic is now an unrelated event that might derail one project activity.

Changing the subject line to reflect a shift in subject can help everyone keep an email conversation focused as its topics evolve. This attention to detail can dramatically set you apart as a considerate businessperson who's on the ball.

PRACTICE 5.4

How much attention do you pay to your subject lines? Do you usually stop to consider whether each one accurately describes and previews your email? Can you think of a time when you forgot to change the subject line when you replied to a message but changed the topic?

Proofread your message

Some people believe that a professional writing style isn't important for email — that the rules of grammar, punctuation, and spelling don't apply. Let's look closely at that belief.

Suppose you received the following message from someone you'd never met. What image would you form of the person who wrote it?

> Dear Supplier Partner:
>
> I am pleased to announce: that InfoSearch has adcepted a offer, from Online Libary, Inc. to purchase it's website. Marcus Wellenby, Onlines CEO and I have work non-stop in recent weeks to put the deal together with minimum affects for both customers and our supplier partners. This will inable the InfoSearch.com web site to contine to operate and, give it a chance to realize it's potential.
>
> I want to apologize to any of you who have had a difficulty, in contacting us while we have operated with a skeletel staff in anticipation of this transatcion. I also want to personnelly thank you. For your support and for a wonderful asociation to those of you I have the pleasure of meeting.
>
> Best Regrds,
>
> Suzanne Boyles

Typos and nonstandard English can distract readers from the message by reminding them of the mechanics of writing. Careful, correct English focuses a message and shows consideration by removing these distractions.

We believe that error-free email is important. Remember these key points:

- The email you write conveys a particular image to your readers. If your grammar, punctuation, and spelling become sloppy, then your image may suffer.

- Some careless writing and errors will mislead readers or make it difficult for them to understand what you're trying to say.

Before you send out an email, do yourself and your readers a favor by proofreading it. The process doesn't take long, and it promotes a considerate, positive, professional image of you and your organization.

APPLY WHAT YOU'VE LEARNED

To complete this chapter, look back to the writing plan you wrote out on pages 56 and 57. Write a draft of your email below, applying the techniques from Lesson 2 (such as the journalistic triangle), Lesson 3 (such as lists), and this lesson (such as techniques for the CC line and subject line).

TO:

CC:

SUBJECT:

MESSAGE TEXT:

PRACTICE WITH
A WRITING WORKSHEET

Two writing worksheets are on the following pages. Use them to try out everything you've learned in this course:

- You can draft a document by using the writing plan you completed at the end of Lesson 1, on pages 56 and 57.

- Or try writing with a new situation in mind, using a worksheet to develop a new writing plan with a scenario from the following table as a framework for your writing plan. Choose whichever scenario below is the best fit for the work you do.

WRITER	Purpose: to inform	Purpose: to persuade
Supervisor communicating internally	To deploy a business plan	To adopt a new approach
Supervisor communicating externally	To change an account representative	To sell a PR campaign
Individual contributor communicating internally	To introduce a new HR system or process	To ask for a favor
Individual contributor communicating externally	To report on meeting details	To suggest a large lunch meeting

WRITING WORKSHEET #1

Subject:

1. **LOOK AT WHAT YOU'RE GOING TO WRITE FROM THE POINT OF VIEW OF YOUR READER OR READERS.**

Name or describe your reader(s): _____

_____

_____

_____

Think about the needs, interests, and concerns of your reader or readers. Then check the appropriate boxes:

Is your reader …

❑ Expecting to hear from you?

❑ Familiar with the subject?

❑ Already interested in what you have to say?

❑ Likely to consider you an authority on the subject?

❑ Likely to find what you have to say useful?

❑ Familiar with your views on the subject?

❑ Already committed to a point of view?

❑ Likely to agree with your point of view?

❑ Likely to find your message uncomfortable?

❑ (Add any other relevant needs, interests, and concerns.)

2. **DECIDE ON YOUR PRIMARY PURPOSE:**

❑ **TO PERSUADE**   ❑ **TO INFORM**

3.   COMPOSE A KEY SENTENCE THAT EXPRESSES YOUR MOST IMPORTANT MESSAGE:

I want my reader(s) to do or to know …

_____

_____

_____

_____

_____

4.   LIST THE FACTS AND IDEAS TO INCLUDE:

_____

_____

_____

_____

_____

_____

_____

_____

_____

_____

_____

_____

_____

_____

_____

_____

5. **GROUP YOUR IDEAS INTO CATEGORIES, AND ADD ANY HEADINGS OR LISTS YOU'LL INCLUDE:**

_____

_____

_____

_____

_____

_____

_____

_____

_____

_____

_____

_____

_____

_____

_____

_____

_____

_____

_____

_____

_____

_____

_____

_____

WRITING WORKSHEET #2

Subject:

1. **LOOK AT WHAT YOU'RE GOING TO WRITE FROM THE POINT OF VIEW OF YOUR READER OR READERS.**

Name or describe your reader(s): _____

_____

_____

_____

Think about your the needs, interests, and concerns of your reader or readers. Then check the appropriate boxes below:

Is your reader ...

- ❏ Expecting to hear from you?
- ❏ Familiar with the subject?
- ❏ Already interested in what you have to say?
- ❏ Likely to consider you an authority on the subject?
- ❏ Likely to find what you have to say useful?
- ❏ Familiar with your views on the subject?
- ❏ Already committed to a point of view?
- ❏ Likely to agree with your point of view?
- ❏ Likely to find your message uncomfortable?
- ❏ (Add any other relevant needs, interests, and concerns.)

2. **DECIDE ON YOUR PRIMARY PURPOSE:**

❏ **TO PERSUADE**   ❏ **TO INFORM**

3. **COMPOSE A KEY SENTENCE THAT EXPRESSES YOUR MOST IMPORTANT MESSAGE:**

I want my reader(s) to do or to know …

_____

_____

_____

_____

_____

4. **LIST THE FACTS AND IDEAS TO INCLUDE:**

_____

_____

_____

_____

_____

_____

_____

_____

_____

_____

_____

_____

_____

_____

_____

_____

_____

_____

5. **GROUP YOUR IDEAS INTO CATEGORIES, AND ADD ANY HEADINGS OR LISTS YOU'LL INCLUDE:**

_____

_____

_____

_____

_____

_____

_____

_____

_____

_____

_____

_____

_____

_____

_____

_____

_____

_____

_____

_____

_____

_____

_____

_____

Congratulations: you've completed this workbook!

Sources

- Einsohn, Amy. *The Copyeditor's Handbook: A Guide for Publishing and Corporate Communications, with Exercises and Answer Keys.* Berkeley: University of California Press, 2006.
- Turabian, Kate L. *A Manual for Writers of Research Papers, Theses, and Dissertations.* 7th ed. Chicago: University of Chicago Press, 2007.
- Williams, Joseph M. *Style: The Basics of Clarity and Grace.* 3rd ed. New York: Pearson Longman, 2009.

About Write It Well

Write It Well began in 1979 as Advanced Communication Designs, Inc. We're a firm of trainers and professional-development consultants who help people in business communicate more efficiently and effectively. We provide practical, job-relevant information, techniques, and strategies that readers and training participants can apply right away to the documents they produce and presentations they deliver for their jobs.

Individuals, teams, training specialists, instructors in corporations and businesses of all sizes, nonprofit organizations, government agencies, and colleges and universities use our books and training programs. The Write It Well Series on Business Communication includes the self-paced training workbooks *Develop and Deliver Effective Presentations*; *Effective Email*; *Land the Job: Writing Effective Resumes and Cover Letters*; *Reports, Proposals, and Procedures*; and *Writing Performance Reviews*. Visit writeitwell.com for more information about our company and detailed descriptions of our publications.

About the Author

Natasha Terk is the author of The Write It Well Series on Business Communication. As the managing director of Write It Well, she leads the firm's business operations and strategy.

Natasha holds master's degrees from the University of San Francisco and the University of Manchester, UK. She has served as a program officer at the Packard Foundation and as a management consultant with La Piana Consulting, and she serves on the board of the Ronald McDonald House of San Francisco.

Natasha has taught business writing at the University of California, Berkeley, and been a consultant for Berkeley's Haas School of Business. She leads on-site and online webinars and workshops for clients including Hewlett-Packard, Granite Construction, IKEA, National Semiconductor, and the Port of Oakland. She gives keynote speeches and presentations on business communications at seminars and large conferences.

Lightning Source UK Ltd.
Milton Keynes UK
UKOW01f1024170215

246417UK00004B/60/P